Build Your Own DECK

The cost of labor and materials is rising constantly. People are turning to do-it-yourself projects as a means of completing additions and renovations to their houses. If you are a homeowner, a deck significantly increases the value of your property. This book will enable you to make a new deck a reality if you follow the instructions carefully. Should you ever decide to sell your home, a carefully planned and constructed deck will add considerably to your home's resale value.

Build Your Own Deck Manual is a unique guide that concentrates on the process of building rather than designing the deck. Certainly all the elements of design and proper plan detailing are considered, but this is foremost a book that graphically demonstrates the latest in deck construction techniques. Each step of the construction process is illustrated in detail. Several design alternatives are presented for your consideration.

You will understand the construction terminology used in this book as you progress. A Deck Glossary is provided on pages 44 and 45 to explain unfamiliar terms. Study the cutaway drawings and captions shown on pages 4 and 5 to help you envision your deck. On pages 47-77 select from a wide range of predesigned deck plans available for ordering at any time.

Every effort has been made at the time of publication to ensure the accuracy of the information contained herein. However, the reader should check for his or her own assurance and must be responsible for design, selection and use of suppliers, materials and actual construction.

No part of this work covered by the copyright herein may be reproduced or used in any form or by any means - graphic, electronic, or mechanical, including photocopying, recording, taping, or information storage retrieval system - for any purpose other than the purchaser's personal use without the written permission of HDA, Inc. Happy deck building!

Build Your Own Deck Manual is published by HDA, Inc., 944 Anglum Road, St. Louis, MO 63042. All rights reserved. Reproduction in whole or in part without written permission of the publisher is prohibited. Printed in the U.S.A. © 1998. Artist drawings and photos shown in this publication may vary slightly from the actual working drawings. Some photos are shown in mirror reverse. Please refer to the floor plan for accurate layout.

Copyright All plans appearing in this publication are protected under copyright law. Reproduction of the illustrations or working drawings by any means is strictly prohibited. The right of building only one structure from the plans purchased is licensed exclusively to the buyer and the plans may not be resold unless by express written authorization.

For more information on HDA, Inc. and our products please visit www.houseplansandmore.com and www.projectplans.com.

Current Printing (last digit) 5 4 3 2 1
ISBN-13: 978-0-934039-48-2
ISBN-10: 0-934039-48-8

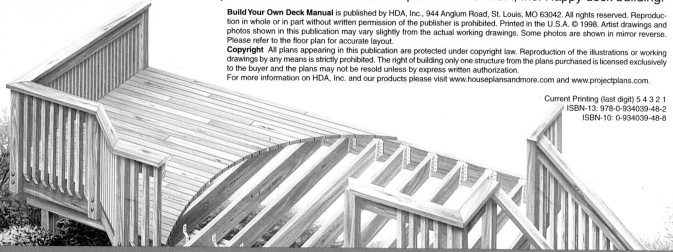

TABLE OF CONTENTS

Build Your Own Deck?

The answer is YES! By planning and doing all or part of the work yourself, you can have the deck you might not otherwise be able to afford. By supplying the labor and buying materials yourself, construction costs can be cut significantly.

Framing out a deck is not difficult. Standardized materials and construction techniques make it relatively easy if you take time to plan and work carefully.

Planning Your Deck

The key to a successful deck project is planning! Once you have begun construction of your deck, it is both costly and time-consuming to correct errors. So the motto of the Do-It-Yourself deck builder must be **PLAN AHEAD!** Whether you choose to draw the plans for your deck following the guidelines in this manual or you decide to purchase a pre-drawn deck plan that can be adapted to your specific requirements, you must carefully plan all elements of your deck project.

Read all the techniques and tips in this book carefully before you begin construction. It will help you determine the work you can handle alone and also where expert help might be needed. You can also learn many construction basics by studying existing decks.

Here is a checklist of design information which you must gather before you begin to design your deck:

- **Local Building Requirements -** Visit your local building department and determine how local building codes and zoning ordinances will influence your project. Be prepared to apply for a building permit once you have completed your design.

- **Deed Restrictions -** Are there conditions in your property deed that restrict the type and location of your deck? Are you planning to place your deck over property controlled by an easement for right-of-way or utility access?

- **Climatic Factors -** You need to determine specific climatic conditions on your property. For example, what is the maximum soil frost depth at your site? What is the prevailing wind direction during the season when your deck will receive maximum use? How much snow load will your deck have to carry during the winter months? Finally, evaluate the microclimate of your intended deck location. Microclimate includes the shading effects of deciduous or evergreen trees and shrubs, the angle of the sun in relation to nearby landscaping during different seasons, soil drainage conditions, and prevailing wind and temperature conditions.

- **Deck Functions -** What do you want your deck to do? Will it serve as an extension of a room in your home? Do you see your deck as a social gathering spot or as a place of seclusion from your neighbors? Do you want it to perform a special function such as containing a built-in barbecue or supporting a portable spa or hot tub?

- **Your Budget -** You must determine an estimated dollar amount that you plan to spend on your deck. Do you plan to construct it yourself or will you subcontract with a professional to build the deck after you have purchased materials? Perhaps you want a contractor to complete your deck project in its entirety. It is helpful if you can set upper and lower spending limits so that you can consider options in the materials that you plan for your deck. If you decide to finance your deck project, don't forget to include interest cost in the total cost amount.

- **Your Materials Source -** After you have completed your design work and have settled on a bill of materials, you should remember that your local lumber chain or home improvement store is an invaluable resource for the completion of your project. Consult with your local store to check for the materials you require. If special ordering is necessary, determine lead times for the materials. Don't underestimate the importance of a reputable resource like your local home improvement store in providing both quality materials and design knowledge.

Planning Your Deck

The deck site plans on this page are included to exemplify how your deck can serve as an extension of the living space in your home. Consider first how you want to access your deck – which rooms in particular should provide entry to your deck space. Do you currently have enough door openings to handle the traffic on your deck? Perhaps you need to install additional patio doors to provide more than one access point.

If you are planning a deck that is attached to your home, you must carefully evaluate the use of door and window openings to integrate the deck with your home. Multiple access points open your deck to the interior living space of your home. For example, Figure 3A illustrates a wrap-around deck that you can access from the dining room or the sun room area.

If you are fortunate enough to be able to construct a large deck like those illustrated in Figures 3B and 3C, you will increase the total usable living area of your home significantly by careful planning and deck design. These decks add extremely useful square footage that can serve multiple functions – a simple recreation space, an outdoor dining and entertainment area, or a happy place to get away and relax.

Decks provide a sense of openness to the living space of your home. However, you can also create an enclosed, private environment with a deck that adjoins two exterior walls. In Figure 3D, observe how the modest rectangular deck links the living room and the family room while the walls of those rooms provide protection from the elements and privacy.

Figure 3B

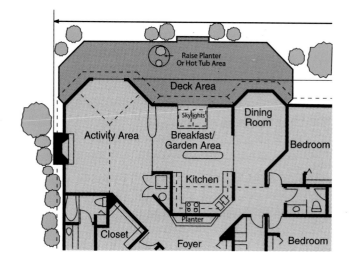

Figure 3C

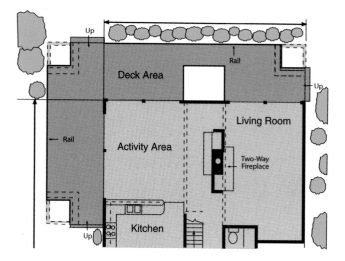

Figure 3A

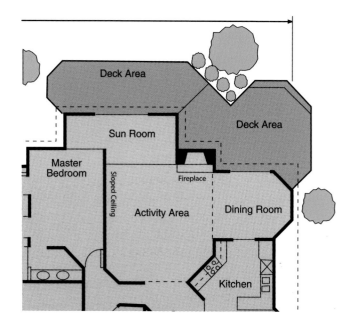

Figure 3D

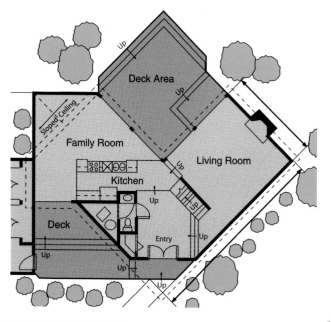

Anatomy of a Deck

Basic Pier Block Deck

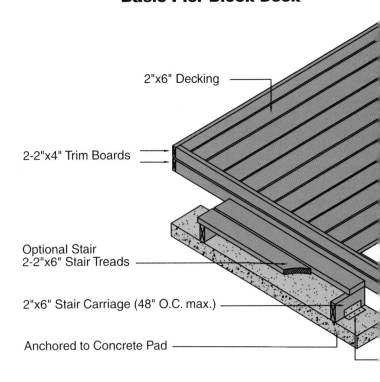

2"x6" Decking

2-2"x4" Trim Boards

Optional Stair
2-2"x6" Stair Treads

2"x6" Stair Carriage (48" O.C. max.)

Anchored to Concrete Pad

Standard Level Deck

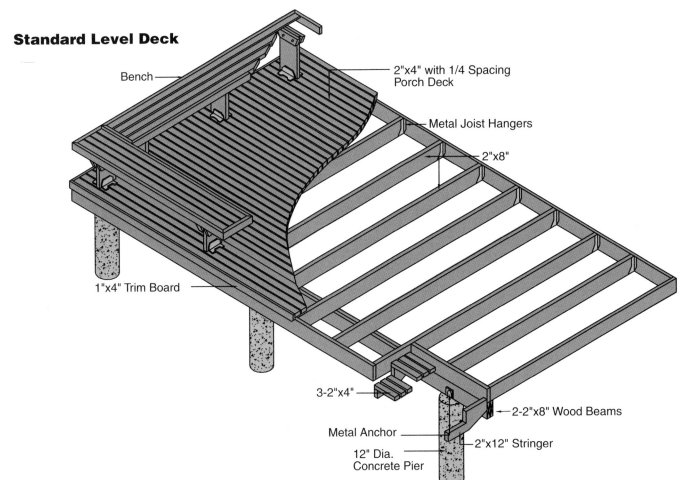

Bench

1"x4" Trim Board

2"x4" with 1/4 Spacing
Porch Deck

Metal Joist Hangers

2"x8"

3-2"x4"

Metal Anchor

12" Dia.
Concrete Pier

2"x12" Stringer

2-2"x8" Wood Beams

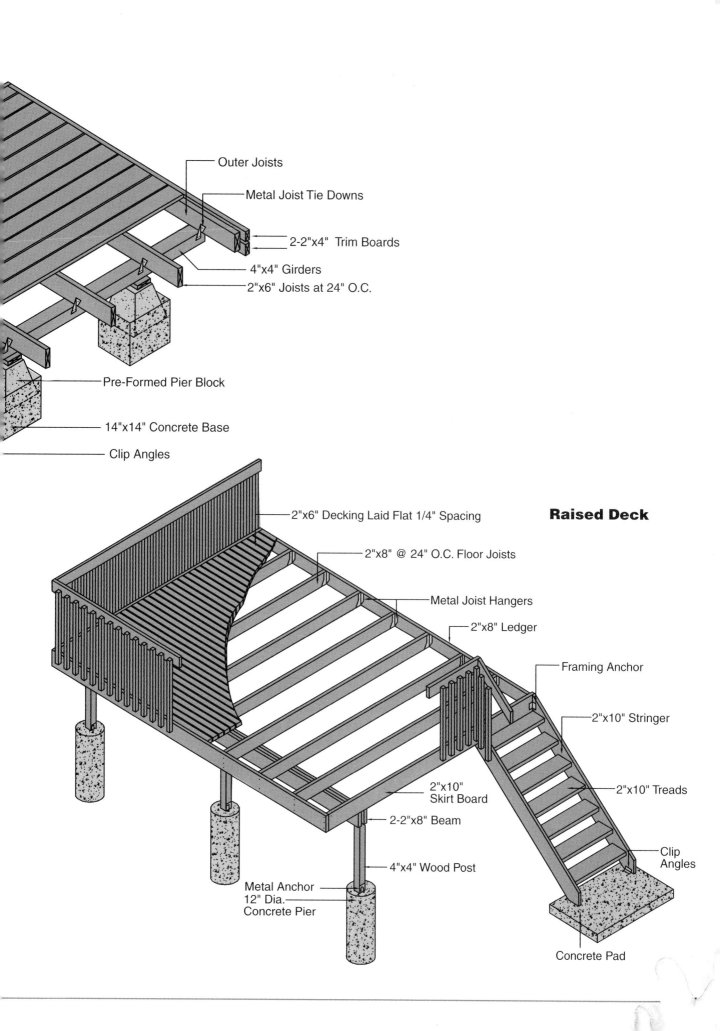

Outer Joists

Metal Joist Tie Downs

2-2"x4" Trim Boards

4"x4" Girders

2"x6" Joists at 24" O.C.

Pre-Formed Pier Block

14"x14" Concrete Base

Clip Angles

2"x6" Decking Laid Flat 1/4" Spacing

Raised Deck

2"x8" @ 24" O.C. Floor Joists

Metal Joist Hangers

2"x8" Ledger

Framing Anchor

2"x10" Stringer

2"x10" Treads

2"x10" Skirt Board

Clip Angles

2-2"x8" Beam

4"x4" Wood Post

Metal Anchor
12" Dia.
Concrete Pier

Concrete Pad

Basic Deck Designs

Low-Level Attached Deck
Plan #DM2-107D-3002

Multi-Level Attached Deck
Plan #DM2-107D-3001

Expandable Decks
Plan #DM2-002D-3002

Multi-Level Detached Deck
Plan #DM2-002D-3009

Free-Standing Low-Level Deck
Plan #DM2-002D-3021

Multi-Level Raised Deck
Plan #DM2-002D-3020

Deck With Attached Gazebo
Plan #DM2-002D-3029

Low-Level Shaded Deck
Plan #DM2-002D-3025

Drawing a Plan for Your Deck

Obtain the Correct Drawing Tools

Pre-drawn plans are available starting on page 48. These drawings include all the necessary information needed when building your deck. If you prefer to try your hand at designing a deck of your own, the tools you will need to draw plans for your deck are available at your local craft, art supply or variety store. You should obtain a transparent plastic ruler to help you keep your drawings to scale. Scale is a system of representation in plan drawing where small dimensions represent an equivalent large dimension. Scale is typically expressed as an equation such as 1/4"=1'-0". Better than a simple ruler is an architect's scale that calibrates dimensions directly to the scale used on your drawing. You can read 5'-0" at 1/4" scale directly on the architect's scale rather than multiplying 5 x 1-1/4" and measuring to scale with your ruler.

Also purchase two transparent right angle triangles that help to measure angles and keep your work square. You should obtain a 6"-45 degree triangle and a 6"-30/60 degree triangle. Use a medium lead pencil to draw your plans and have an eraser at hand – you will need it to correct inevitable revisions. We have provided graph paper in this manual at two different scales for your convenience. Finally, you'll need a 25-foot measuring tape to obtain outside dimensions that you will draw to scale in your deck plans.

Measuring the Site

With your 25-foot measuring tape you can begin to measure the site. Place construction stakes at the perimeter of your imaginary deck. If you are building an attached deck, use the house wall as an initial reference point. Then start to transfer measurements from your deck outline to paper. It is standard practice to orient your base plan drawing with north at the top of the plan. You should include on your base plan all surrounding elements which could influence the final design of your deck – paths or doorways which will provide access to the deck, deck views and privacy considerations, trees and their shadow patterns, other buildings, grade conditions, and any nearby underground utility services.

Finalizing the Design

Once you have transferred your site measurements into the base plan, you can begin to use the base plan to help you create the final drawings for your deck. Carefully study all the elements of the base plan and resolve any final decisions concerning deck size, height, placement, and type of pier construction.

Figure 7 - Side View of Deck Framing

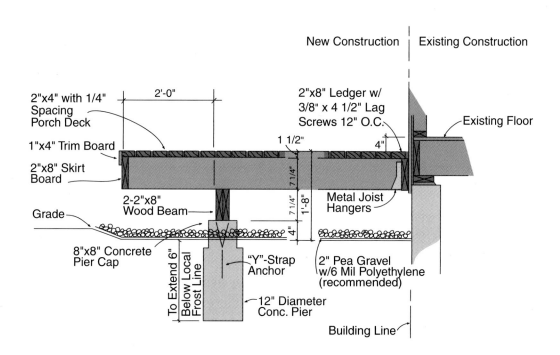

Drawing a Plan for Your Deck

Pier Location Plan

Once you have decided on a final design, you first need to draw a pier location plan that shows the exact placement of the piers in relation to the deck outline and the existing structure if you are building an attached deck. Consult the span charts on pages 10-11 to be certain that your piers are not spaced too far apart for the joist and beam spacing that you have selected.

Deck Framing Plan

Based on the pier location plan, you will draw a deck framing plan that shows exact measurements for the joists and girders on your deck. Some designers find it easier to draw one plan for joist framing and another for girder framing. Remember to consult the table of nominal versus actual dimensions of dimensional lumber (see chart on page 16) when you calculate exact lengths of joists and girders. Again consult the span charts on pages 10-11 to ensure that you have not exceeded maximum design values for joist and girder spans.

Deck Plan

Using your deck framing plan, draw the surface of your deck as it will appear in a bird's eye view from the top. This plan will help you estimate the amount of decking (see chart on page 15), railing, and stair material required to complete your deck.

Deck Elevations

You've drawn the layers of your deck construction from the top view when you made the pier location plan, deck framing plan, and deck plan. Using those top-view plans as a guide, you then draw your deck in a sideways view – as deck elevations, which show your deck as it will appear from front, back, left, and rear sides.

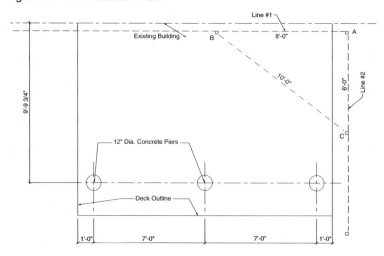

Figure 8A - Pier Location Plan

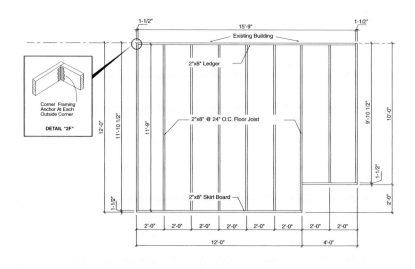

Figure 8B - Deck Framing Plan

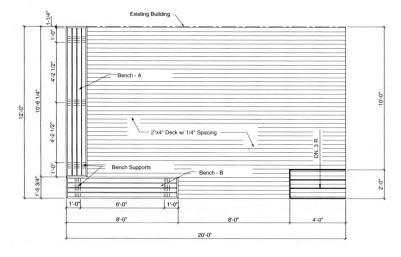

Figure 8C - Deck Plan

Planning the Deck Substructure

Once you have drawn the surface of your deck in a plan view, you must design the deck's supporting substructure. The tables on pages 10-11 will assist you in planning the critical substructure system of your deck. You should be aware that these tables reflect spans and spacings for a total load of 60 pounds per square foot, which in many localities is the current load requirement for decks mandated by the Uniform Building Code. The total load of 60 P.S.F. has two component loads – the first of 10 P.S.F. "dead" load plus a second of 50 P.S.F. "live" load. While the 60 P.S.F. total load is more than adequate for most substructure designs, special circumstances such as heavy snow loads or the weight of a hot tub will require consultation with a design professional.

Your own local building department may or may not support the 60 P.S.F. total load requirement. Again we strongly advise you to consult with your local building department to ensure that your deck substructure will meet local codes.

How to Use Deck Spans and Spacings Tables

Use the tables on pages 10-11 to plan the substructure of your deck. First determine the species group of the lumber you will use to build the substructure of your deck. If you are planning to use two different lumber species (such as Douglas fir for joists and redwood for posts, beams, and decking), don't forget to use the correct species group in each appropriate chart.

Refer to the illustrated dimensions in Figure 9 below as a graphic guide to the dimensions listed in the tables. For example, Dimension "A" refers to the maximum allowable span for decking boards listed in the Decking Span Table. Dimension "B" measures both joist span and beam spacing which are different names for an identical dimension. Dimension "C" reflects beam spans for a given beam size. Dimension "D" shows the minimum post size required to support a given load area (which you calculate by multiplying). Dimension "B" by Dimension "C"). Remember that these spans are for solid beams rather than built-up beams. A 4x6 beam (measuring 3-1/2" x 5-1/2") has greater load carrying strength than a beam built from nailing together two 2x6s (measuring 3" x 5-1/2").

Design the Substructure CAREFULLY

In planning the substructure of your deck, remember that you are working with a complex set of variables and that your final design will reflect a choice between competing alternatives. For example, if you increase the number of concrete piers you can reduce joist spans and girder size and spans. However, if your local frost line requires that piers be constructed to a depth of 3 feet, you might want to reduce the number of piers and increase joist and beam spans. Determine a solution that is cost-effective but does not compromise the strength and durability of your deck. A deck that is inadequately supported by its substructure is dangerous and will require costly repairs at a later date.

Figure 9 - Deck Substructure

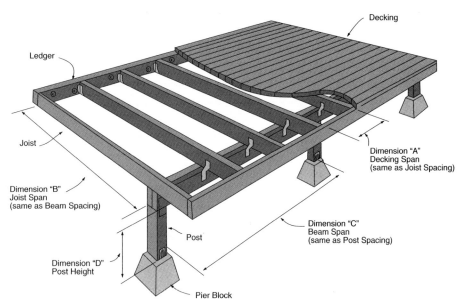

Deck Spans and Spacings

Charts are Based on a 60 P.S.F. Total Load
50 P.S.F. Live Load Plus 10 P.S.F. Dead Load

Strength Groups of Common Softwoods Species

Group I	Group II	
Douglas Fir Hemlock Western Larch Western Pine Southern Spruce	Cedar, Western Douglas Fir (South) Fir (White, Alpine) Hemlock (Eastern, Mountain) Pine (Eastern White, Idaho White, Lodgepole) Pine (Northern, Ponderosa, Red, Sugar, Western White) Redwood Spruce (Eastern, Engelmann)	

Decking Span Chart

Maximum Allowable Span
See Dimension "A" on Page 9
Based on 1200 P.S.F. Fibre Strength Lumber – Construction Grade (No. 2) or Better.

Species Group	Laid Flat		Laid On Edge	
	1x4, 1x6, 5/4x6￼ (S4S, T&G, Radius Edge)	All 2x Lumber (Standard and T&G)	2x3 Lumber (Standard)	2x4 Lumber (Standard)
I	16"	60"	90"	144"
II	14"	48"	78"	120"

Joist Span Chart

Maximum Allowable Joist Span
See Dimension "B" on Page 9
Total Load 60 P.S.F. (50 P.S.F. Live Load plus 10 P.S.F. Dead Load)
Based on 1200 P.S.F. Fibre Strength Lumber – Construction Grade (No. 2) or Better.

Species Group	Joist Size	Maximum Allowable Joist Span		
		Joist Spacing 16"	24"	32"
I	2x6	9' - 6"	8' - 3"	7' - 5"
	2x8	12' - 7"	11' - 0"	10' - 0"
	2x10	16' - 1"	14' - 0"	12' - 10"
II	2x6	8' - 4"	7' - 4"	6' - 6"
	2x8	11' - 0"	9' - 8"	8' - 8"
	2x10	14' - 2"	12' - 4"	11' - 2"

Beam Spans and Post Heights

Charts are Based on a 60 P.S.F. Total Load
50 P.S.F. Live Load Plus 10 P.S.F. Dead Load

Beam Spans And Post Heights

Maximum Allowable Beam Spans
See Dimension "C" on Page 9
Total Load 60 P.S.F. (50 P.S.F. Live Load plus 10 P.S.F. Dead Load)
Based on 1200 P.S.F. Fibre Strength Lumber – Construction Grade (No. 2) or Better.
Beams are on edge. Span distance is center to center between posts or supports.

Species Group	Beam Size	Beam Spacing (See Dimension "B")							
		4'	5'	6'	7'	8'	9'	10'	11'
I	4x4	up to 4'							
	4x6	up to 6'							
	3x8	up to 8'			up to 6'				
	4x8	up to 10'	up to 9'	up to 8'	up to 7'	up to 6'			
	3x10	up to 11'	up to 10'	up to 9'	up to 8'	up to 7'	up to 6'		
	4x10	up to 12'	up to 11'	up to 10'	up to 9'	up to 8'	up to 7'		
	3x12		up to 12'	up to 11'	up to 10'	up to 9'		up to 8'	
	4x12			up to 12'		up to 11'	up to 10'	up to 9'	
	6x10					up to 12'	up to 11'	up to 10'	
	6x12						up to 12'		
II	4x4	up to 4'							
	4x6	up to 6'							
	3x8	up to 7'		up to 6'					
	4x8	up to 9'	up to 8'	up to 7'		up to 6'			
	3x10	up to 10'	up to 9'	up to 8'	up to 7'		up to 6'		
	4x10	up to 11'	up to 10'	up to 9'	up to 8'		up to 7'		up to 6'
	3x12	up to 12'	up to 11'	up to 10'	up to 9'	up to 8'		up to 7'	
	4x12		up to 12'	up to 11'	up to 10'		up to 9'	up to 8'	
	6x10			up to 12'	up to 11'	up to 10'	up to 9'		
	6x12				up to 12'		up to 11'	up to 10'	

Minimum Post Heights
See Dimension "D" on Page 9
(Wood Beam Supports)

Species Group	Beam Size	Load Area = Beam Spacing (Dim. "B") x Post Spacing (Dim. "C") in Square Feet								
		36 LBS.	40 LBS.	60 LBS.	72 LBS.	84 LBS.	96 LBS.	108 LBS.	120 LBS.	132 LBS.
I	4x4	up to 12' heights		up to 10' heights	up to 8' heights					
	4x6					up to 12' heights		up to 10' heights		
	6x6									up to 12' heights
II	4x4	up to 12' heights	up to 10' heights	up to 8' heights						
	4x6			up to 12' heights	up to 10' heights					
	6x6					up to 12' heights				

Planning Your Deck Surface

The deck surface is your deck's most visible element and the one that you will have to live with intimately as you use your deck. So careful planning of your deck surface is in order. If cost and ease of construction are your primary considerations, then you should stick with the classic pattern of parallel 2x6s laid perpendicular to the joists (see Figure 12A). However, if expense is not the primary consideration and you have modest construction experience, you should consider some of the other decking patterns illustrated to the right in Figures 12B-12F.

You should be aware that diagonal decking patterns require closer joist spacing to support longer decking spans when deck boards run diagonal to joists. Consequently, you must plan your deck surface in coordination with planning your deck substructure. As a rule of thumb, a complicated deck surface pattern requires a more complex and costly deck substructure.

A simpler yet visually interesting alternative to diagonal decking is to alternate widths of 2x dimensional lumber laid flat. See page 13 for patterns you can create by alternating 2x2s, 2x4s, and 2x6s.

You can design a deck surface with 2x3s or 2x4s on edge rather than laid flat. On edge decking is far more expensive than decking laid flat but can span much longer distances between joists.

The modular checkerboard pattern illustrated in Figure 12E offers bold visual impact and is not as difficult to construct as diagonal decking. However, the squares must be carefully laid out in advance so that support spacings correspond to the dimensions of the square. Extra blocking is often required so that the end of each decking board is directly supported.

Whatever deck pattern you select, space decking boards at least 3/16" for proper drainage, ventilation, and the natural shrinkage and swelling of wood.

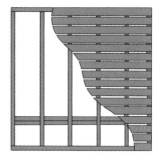

Figure 12A - Standard parallel 2x6s. This pattern is the easiest to construct of all the decking patterns.

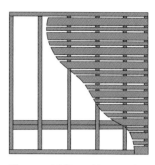

Figure 12B - Alternating 2x4s and 2x6s. This pattern provides visual interest while retaining simplicity of construction.

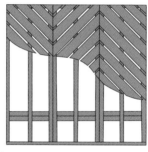

Figure 12C - Herringbone 2x6s. More difficult to construct but offers a striking visual effect.

Figure 12D - Diagonal 2x6s. Decrease joist spacing to provide additional support for diagonal decking.

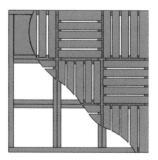

Figure 12E - Checkerboard pattern offers visual impact with relative ease of construction.

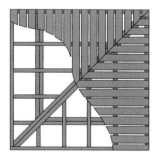

Figure 12F - L-Pattern which sets decking perpendicular to joists but requires complex deck substructure.

Planning Your Deck Surface

**Three examples of varying
the widths of decking lumber in
order to create a dramatic visual effect:**

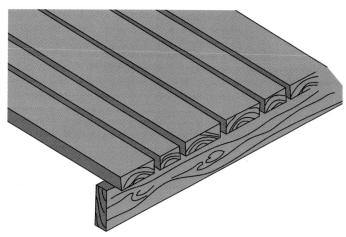

Figure 13A - 2x6 and 2x4 Wood Members

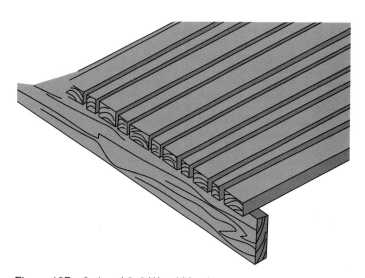

Figure 13B - 2x4 and 2x2 Wood Members

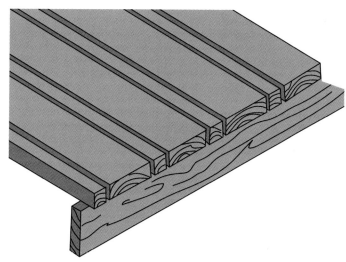

Figure 13C - 2x6 and 2x2 Wood Members

Choosing Lumber for Your Deck

Choosing The Correct Lumber

Choosing the correct lumber for your deck can be as consequential as determining the correct design. For use in a deck, the lumber you select must perform well in an exposed outdoor environment. Performance is measured according to the following criteria:

Freedom from Shrinkage and Warping - Lumber that has dimensional stability will not cause problems later. You don't want to have to replace deck boards only 2 or 3 years after construction.

Hardness - Gives your deck durability and prevents marring of the deck surface if sharp objects are dropped.

Decay Resistance - Generally lumber cut from the heartwood (center of the log) is more resistant to decay than lumber cut from sapwood (outside of the log). However, chemical pressure-treatment can provide decay resistance to species that lack this property.

Workability - Refers to the ease with which you can saw, nail, or shape lumber.

Nail Holding - Determines whether or not a given species possesses good nail-holding power.

Paint Holding - The ability to hold a finish. Some species which contain high levels of natural extractives (such as pitch or resins) do not hold a finish well.

Fire Resistance - All woods are combustible, but some resist fire better than others. Woods that do not contain large amounts of resin are relatively slow to ignite.

Strength and Weight - Wood that is relatively light in weight but possesses great strength is ideal.

Choosing The Species Of Wood

While no single species performs ideally according to all of the criteria, your local lumber dealer will be able to advise you regarding the lumber species most suited to your area. Often you must balance considerations of economy with performance. For example, redwood is considered a premium decking material, but high transportation costs outside the area of manufacture make pressure-treated pine woods a more economical alternative. Here is a concise guide to some common softwood lumber species used in deck construction:

Cedar, Western Red - Popular for the durability and decay-resistance of its heartwood.

Cypress - Cypress resists decay, has an attractive reddish coloration, and holds paint well.

Douglas Fir, Larch - Douglas fir has great strength and is used best in the substructure of your deck, especially in the joist members.

Pines - Numerous pine species have excellent workability but must be pressure-treated for use in deck construction.

Southern Pine - Unlike the soft pines described above, southern pines possess strength but are only moderately decay and warp resistant.

Poplar - Has moderate strength, resists decay and warping.

Redwood - The premium decking material because of its durability, resistance to decay, and beautiful natural brownish-red coloration.

Spruce - Typically spruce species are readily available but do not have great decay resistance.

Choosing Lumber for Your Deck

Remember that in certain circumstances you can use two different species of lumber to construct your deck. For example, redwood can be used for decking and post members while Douglas fir is used for strength in the deck joists and girders.

Whatever lumber species you select, study the illustrations to the right to learn the difference between the grain patterns in dimensional lumber. Flat grain lumber is cut with the grain parallel to the face of the board. Typically used for decking, flat grain boards should be used with the bark-side up in order to minimize cupping and grain separation. Vertical grain lumber, a more expensive grade used for finish work, is cut with the grain perpendicular to the face of the board.

The illustration to the right will give you an idea of some of the defects found in dimensional lumber. Typical defects are **checks** that result from separation of wood across annual rings, **knots** that result from a portion of a tree branch incorporated into cut lumber, and **splits** which are a separation of the wood due to tearing apart of wood cells. A **shake** is a lengthwise separation of the wood that usually occurs between the rings of annual growth. None of the above defects should cause you to reject lumber outright. However, wood with a **bow, cup, crook, wane, split** or **twist** should be avoided in deck construction.

Dimensional lumber is typically sold in incremental lengths of 8, 10, 12, 14, 16 and 20 feet. When you plan your deck, you should try to consider standard board lengths in the overall dimensions of your deck. A 12' x 16' deck (192 sq. ft.) will be far more economical to build than a deck measuring 11' x 18' (198 sq. ft.) due to wastage.

The chart at right shows you how many decking boards to purchase for a given deck width in feet. If your deck is greater than 16 or 20 feet in length, however, you will need to purchase at least two different board lengths for every run of decking.

Figure 15C - Lumber Sizes

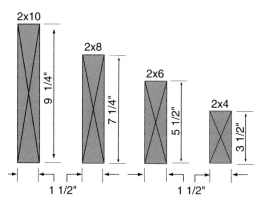

Figure 15A - Grain Location

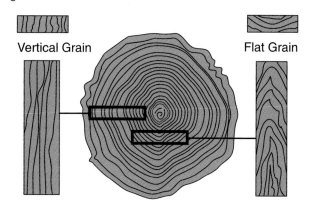

Figure 15B - Lumber Defects

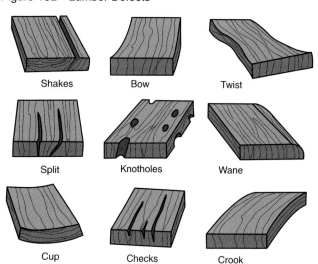

Deck Boards Required For A Given Deck Width (in feet)

Deck Width	2x4s Laid Flat	2x6s Laid Flat	2xs On Edge
8	26	16	56
9	29	18	63
10	33	21	71
11	36	23	78
12	39	25	85
13	42	27	92
14	46	29	99
15	49	31	106
16	52	33	113
17	56	35	120
18	59	37	127
19	62	39	134
20	66	42	142
21	69	44	149
22	72	46	156
23	75	48	163
24	79	50	170

Choosing Lumber for Your Deck

Remember that the nominal dimensions of lumber do not indicate the actual finished size of dimensional lumber. For example, a 2x6 decking board measures approximately 1-1/2" x 5-1/2" depending upon moisture content and surface. Lumber that has a rough surface will measure close to the nominal size in comparison to lumber that is surfaced on four sides (known as S4S).

The most critical factor in determining actual sizes of dimensional lumber is the moisture content of the wood. Look for the grade stamp imprinted on lumber to determine moisture content. Typical moisture content ratings are:

MC 15 (less than 15% moisture content)
S-DRY (less than 19% moisture content)
S-GRN (greater than 19% moisture content)

A 2x6 surfaced unseasoned board (S-GRN) will actually measure 1-9/16" x 5-5/8" compared to 1-1/2" x 5-1/2" for a 2x6 rated surfaced dry (S-DRY). The chart at right shows actual versus nominal sizes of dimensional lumber that is S4S and S-DRY or better.

It is wise to avoid unseasoned lumber especially in the selection of your decking. Decking which is unseasoned can shrink considerably as it dries naturally and will leave hazardous gaps over 1/4" between deck boards.

Standard Dimensions of Surfaced Lumber

Nominal Size	Surfaced (Actual) Size
1 x 2	3/4" x 1-1/2"
1 x 3	3/4" x 2-1/2"
1 x 4	3/4" x 3-1/2"
1 x 6	3/4" x 5-1/2"
1 x 8	3/4" x 7-1/4"
1 x 10	3/4" x 9-1/4"
1 x 12	3/4" x 11-1/4"
2 x 3	1-1/2" x 2-1/2"
2 x 4	1-1/2" x 3-1/2"
2 x 6	1-1/2" x 5-1/2"
2 x 8	1-1/2" x 7-1/4"
2 x 10	1-1/2" x 9-1/4"
2 x 12	1-1/2" x 11-1/4"
4 x 4	3-1/2" x 3-1/2"
4 x 10	3-1/2" x 9-1/4"
6 x 8	5-1/2" x 7-1/2"

Ordering Deck Materials

Complete the sample material list on page 17 before you begin to shop. If you are using one of the pre-drawn deck plans offered in the back of this manual, each plan comes with a complete list of materials. If you have designed your own deck, create a material list from the final design after approval by your local building department.

Especially consider the quality and grade of the lumber you are purchasing. Poor quality materials will yield a meager return on your deck investment. Finally, if you are a novice Do-It-Yourselfer, don't forget that a dealer who provides knowledgeable service as well as economical materials can save you from costly and time-consuming errors.

Don't hesitate to order at least a 5-10% overage of materials to make up for inevitable cutting mistakes or lumber defects. Be aware that dimensional lumber is sold either by the board foot, the lineal (or running) foot, or by the piece. A board foot of lumber represents the amount of lumber in a board 1" thick x 12" wide x 12" long. Use the following formula to compute board feet:

$$\text{Board Feet} = \frac{\text{Length (Feet) x Width (Inches) x Thickness (Inches)}}{12}$$

Sample Material List

	Size	Length	Quantity	X	Cost	=	Total Cost
Foundation							
Concrete							
Sand							
Gravel							
Substructure							
Posts							
Girders							
Deck Joists							
Rim Joists							
Ledger							
Bracing							
Fascia/Trim Boards							
Miscellaneous							
Surface Lumber							
Decking							
Stairs							
Stair Stringer							
Stair Riser							
Stair Tread							
Railings							
Railings							
Balusters							
Connectors							
Nails							
Joist Hangers							
Joist Anchors							
Post Base Anchors							
Post Caps							
Lag Bolts w/ Washers							
Screws							
Grand Total							

Nails and Fasteners

Nails are the most common fastener used in deck framing and construction. Nail lengths are indicated by the term penny, noted by a small letter **d**. In most cases, nails increase in diameter as they increase in length. Heavier construction framing is accomplished with common nails. The extra thick shank of the common nail has greater strength than other types. A wide thick head spreads the load and resists pull-through. For the substructure of your deck where nails are hidden, consider vinyl coated sinkers or cement coated nails which bond to the wood and will not pull up as readily as uncoated nails.

To fasten your decking planks to deck joists, use hot-dipped galvanized common nails, typically 10d or longer. To prevent splitting, predrill nail holes through decking. Spiral nails or annular ring nails provide greater holding power and are less likely to pull up with weathering of your deck. If you have selected redwood for decking, avoid poor-quality nails that will react with the decay-resisting substances in the wood and cause unsightly stains. Finally, consider deck screws as the most expensive but most flexible means of fastening your decking. Deck screws will not pull out and easily allow replacement of individual deck boards at a later time.

Box nails are similar in shape to common nails, but they have a slimmer shank that is less likely to split wood. Finishing nails are used in work where you want to counter sink and then cover the nail head.

Screws create neat, strong joints for finished work. Heavy-duty lag screws and lag bolts are useful for heavier framing connections, such as girder-to-post.

Figure 18 - Types of Nails and Screws

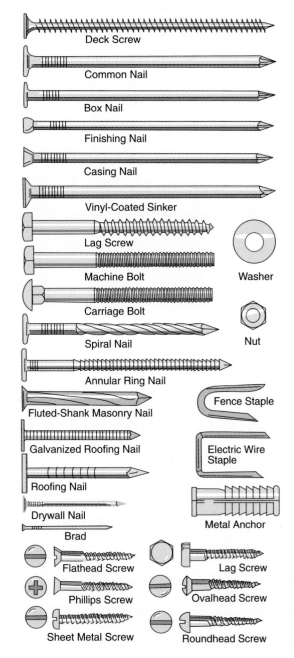

Table of Common Nails

Size	Length	Gauge	# per lb.
2d	1"	15	840
3d	1 1/4"	14	540
4d	1 1/2"	12 1/2	290
5d	1 3/4"	12 1/2	250
6d	2"	11 1/2	160
7d	2 1/4"	11 1/2	150
8d	2 1/2"	10 1/4	100
9d	2 3/4"	10 1/4	90
10d	3"	9	65
12d	3 1/4"	9	60
16d	3 1/2"	8	45
20d	4"	6	30
30d	4 1/2"	5	20
40d	5"	4	16
50d	5 1/2"	3	12
60d	6"	2	10

Finishing Nail Selection Chart

Size	Length	Gauge	# per lb.
2d	1"	16	1000
3d	1 1/4"	15 1/2	870
4d	1 1/2"	15	600
6d	2"	13	310
8d	2 1/2"	12 1/2	190
10d	3"	11 1/2	120

These tables show the approximate number of nails you get in a pound. You'll need more pounds of larger sizes to do a job. For outside jobs, get galvanized or cadmium-plated nails. Aluminum nails are a bit more expensive unless you are doing a smaller project.

Screw Selection Chart

Size	Length	Size	Length
0	1/4-3/8	9	1/2-3
1	1/4-1/2	10	1/2-3 1/2
2	1/4-3/4	11	5/8-3 1/2
3	1/4-1	12	5/8-4
4	1/4-1 1/2	14	3/4-5
5	3/8-1 1/2	16	1-5
6	3/8-2 1/2	18	1 1/4-5
7	3/8-2 1/2	20	1 1/2-5
8	3/8-3	24	3-5

The screw chart shows sizes and the lengths in which they're available. The larger sizes come in longer lengths. Most jobs call for sizes 6-12 in 1/2 to 3 inch lengths. Check size and length before you buy.

Framing With Metal Fasteners

A wide variety of metal fasteners are available to make your deck sturdy and long-lasting. You may be required by local codes to add seismic/hurricane connectors to each joist where it connects to the supporting girder. Post cap connectors and the anchor base connectors illustrated below are a superior means of fastening compared to toenailing. Be certain that connectors are level and square before you secure the post with nails at the nailing holes in the metal connector. Follow the manufacturer's installation instructions.

 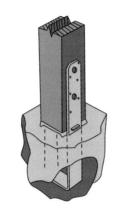 

Figure 19A - Post Base Anchor
Available sizes for: 4x4 Posts, 4x6 Posts, 6x6 Posts

 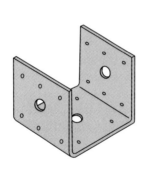

Figure 19B - Post Anchor
Available sizes for: 4x and 6x Posts

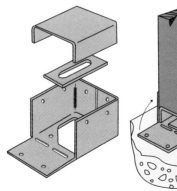 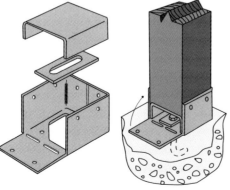

Figure 19C - Adjustable Post Anchor
Available sizes for: 4x4 Posts, 4x6 Posts, 6x6 Posts

Framing With Metal Fasteners

Right-angled corner framing anchors add strength to perpendicular butt joints, especially where rim joists meet. Use joist hangers to attach your deck joists to rim joist members. The modest additional expense of metal fasteners will be more than offset by the added durability of your deck. Remember that metal fasteners help your deck to withstand the expansion and contraction of wood that occurs with changes of season. Secure fasteners using the short ribbed nails provided or where extra strength is required use lag screws in addition to nails.

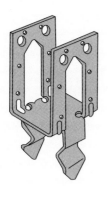
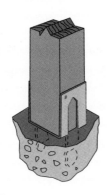

Figure 20A - Post Base
Available sizes for: 4x4 Posts, 4x6 Posts, 6x6 Posts

Figure 20B - Joist Hangers
Available sizes for: 2x4, 2x6, 2x8, 2x10, and 2x12 Joists

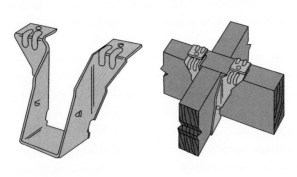

Figure 20C - Beam Frame Connector
Available sizes for: 2x4 Joists and 2x6 Joists

Building Your Deck

Generic Step-By-Step Instructions for Building a Low-Level Attached Deck

1. Site Preparation

Obtain a building permit if required and ensure that you will not be building your deck on top of sewer, gas, or electrical lines that require service. Grade your site and install drainage if necessary.

2. Laying Out the Deck

Mark the position of the deck on your house wall following the deck framing plan. Measure out from the house the depth of your deck and drive a stake to mark each corner. Construct batterboards two feet each way past the outer corners using 2x4 stakes. The top of the batterboards must be level. Extend string lines across the batterboards to outline the deck. Place additional stakes for string lines to locate the top of concrete piers. Each string line should be taut and level. Your outline can also be squared by measuring along one side a distance of 4 feet. Your outline will be square when the diagonal dimension between the two points measures 5 feet. Repeat the process at the opposite corner.

3. Locating Deck Piers

Following the deck framing plan, locate the piers. Place a wood stake in the ground to mark the center of each pier. The string lines you placed above will help you to determine the correct top height for each pier.

4. Determining Height of Deck

In order to determine the height of your deck you must first determine the height of your house floor from your grade line. Once you have determined this height, allow for a 2" to 4" step down from your house floor to the deck so that water will not enter the house. The remaining dimension will be the height of your post from the bottom of the girder to grade line.

5. Attaching the Ledger

Cut ledger to size and brace against the house wall at desired height. Level the ledger with a carpenter's level. Temporarily nail the ledger in place at opposite ends and then recheck for levelness. Once ledger is level, secure to house with 3/8" lag screws that are at least 2" longer than the thickness of the ledger. Use a washer on each fastener and space at 24" maximum intervals.

(continued on page 22)

Building Your Deck

6. Installing Piers and Posts

Dig pier holes 12" in diameter to the necessary depth required by your area. The depth of the hole should be at least half the height of the 4x4 post above ground. Some local codes require that your pier hole extend at least 6 inches below the local frost line. If you are using precast concrete piers, fill the hole with sufficient concrete to embed the pier at least 4" in the concrete and set the pier square and level in its footing. Use the string line to adjust the pier to the correct height. Fasten post base anchor to nailer block on pier.

If you are creating your own pier, build pier forms then fill the hole with concrete. When concrete first starts to set, position a post base anchor in each pier and make sure the post base is centered and level.

Begin to secure 4x4 posts by starting with the lower level post closest to the house. This post will serve as the base post for setting the heights of all other posts. Tie a string line to a nail set flush with the top of the ledger board. Extend the other end of the string over the top of the base post and attach a line level and mark each post at proper height. Cut off excess post. Plumb and square post with a level. Nail posts to post base anchors.

7. Installing the Girders

Cut the girders to their proper lengths following the deck framing plan. Square up corners of girders and be sure all outer edges are in line. Secure girders to posts with post cap connectors.

8. Attaching Joists and Rim Joists

Cut the rim joists to their proper lengths. Attach metal joist hangers to ledger board at 16" or 24" intervals and to opposite rim joist at proper interval. Make certain hangers are square and at proper height. Set the first joist in first hanger on the ledger board. This joist should be level on the top of the girders if you have planned correctly. Install remaining joists in their hangers. Set the rim joist opposite the ledger in place and secure by fastening joists to joist hangers. Secure two additional rim joists to ledger board and opposite rim joist with corner framing anchors. Ensure that all rim joists are square and that deck joists are straight in hangers. Nail deck joists to hangers and use joist ties to fasten joists to girders.

9. Nailing the Decking

Start with the first board along the house wall and allow a 3/8" expansion joint between first board and the wall. Since this first board will serve as a guide for the rest of the decking, place it as square as possible. To prevent against splitting, pre-drill slightly undersized pilot holes at each location where you will fasten decking to the joist. Use three 12 penny hot-dipped galvanized nails at the end of each board and two nails at the joists. Snap a chalk line to keep your nails in a straight line. Use 16 penny nails as spacers for a 3/16" gap between deck boards. When 6 feet of decking remains to be placed, adjust board spacing to avoid a gap at the end of the deck. When all the decking is in place, snap a chalk line along the outside face of the end joists. Cut the deck boards at the chalk line so they're flush with rim joists. Set trim boards flush with decking top and nail to rim joists.

10. Finishing

If you so desire, apply a paint or stain to your finished deck in accordance with manufacturer's instructions provided with the product.

Laying Out the Deck and Locating Piers

Check and recheck your foundation pier layout plan. Errors at this stage are costly and difficult to correct. You must layout the deck and locate piers with accuracy.

Be certain that you know the location of all underground utility and septic lines that may interfere with construction of your deck. Do NOT locate your deck over or near an active septic tank.

Mark the position of your ledger board on your house wall following the deck framing plan. You can either install the ledger (see pages 25-26) temporarily at this time or pencil mark the location and install the ledger later.

Measure out from the house the depth of your deck and drive a stake to mark each corner. Construct batterboards 24" each way past the outer corners using 2x4 stakes as shown below. Drive the stakes holding the batterboards securely into the ground. Use your carpenter's level and a straight 2x4 or a string level on a nylon string to ensure that the tops of the batterboards are level and at the same height as the top of your ledger.

Extend nylon string lines across the batterboards to outline the deck. Each perimeter string should be taut and level. It helps to cut a notch at the top of the batterboard to hold the string line securely in place.

To ensure squareness form a 3-4-5 right triangle with the string lines. Using a felt tipped pen, mark the string line 4 feet out from where the lines intersect. Then mark the other line 3 feet out from the crossing point. Finally measure the distance diagonally between the marks on both string lines. When the distance measures exactly five feet your deck outline is square. Remember that the system of the 3-4-5 right triangle works in any multiple of 3-4-5 such as 6-8-10 or 9-12-15. Repeat this process at each corner of the deck.

Check that your work is square by measuring diagonally from opposite corner marks in an X formation. If your diagonal measurements are equal, your deck perimeter layout is aligned properly. If the measurements are not equal, recheck your work and adjust string lines until they are correct.

Next determine the location for each pier following the deck foundation pier layout plan. Measure along opposite perimeter strings and mark the points that represent the pier centerline(s). Place a stake at these marks and then attach a level string to show the centerline of the piers. This string should be at the same height as the perimeter strings. Mark the location of each pier on the pier centerline string and drop a plumb bob to mark the center of each pier. Identify the center of each pier location with a stake. Place a string for each row of piers.

Figure 23 - Marking Corner Stakes

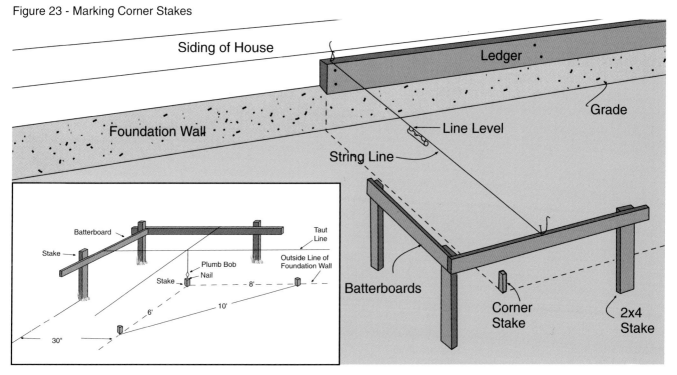

Digging Pier Holes

Dig pier holes 10"-12" in diameter. It's best to move the string lines temporarily before you dig. Depth of pier holes depends upon your local building codes and the level of your local frost line. Use a shovel or post hole digger to dig holes with straight rather than sloping sides. Dig the hole deep enough to allow for 4" of compacted gravel at the bottom of the hole.

Tap the soil at the bottom of the hole to prevent settling of the pier. Add approximately 4" of gravel to the bottom of the hole. At this point you can add reinforcing bar if your local codes require it. The reinforcing bar adds strength to deep concrete piers. The completed hole should be deep enough to allow the top of the completed pier to sit approximately 4"- 6" inches above the finished grade line. Replace string lines and recheck your work.

Figure 24 - Digging Pier Holes

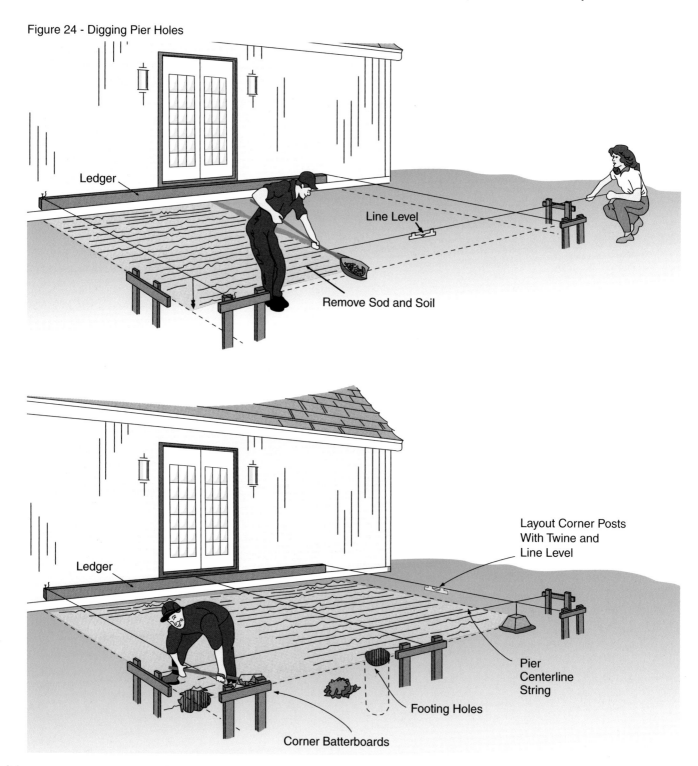

Ledger

Line Level

Remove Sod and Soil

Ledger

Layout Corner Posts With Twine and Line Level

Pier Centerline String

Footing Holes

Corner Batterboards

Attaching the Ledger Board to Your Home

Study the illustrations below and on page 26 which demonstrate different methods of attaching a ledger board to the outside wall of your home.

1. Select only a straight board which is either pressure-treated or cut from a decay resistant species such as redwood or cedar for your ledger. You don't want the ledger to warp or decay and cause severe problems at a later date.

2. Position the ledger so that you step down from the house onto the deck. If the ledger board is higher than your house floor, water can run into the house from the deck. Remember that you will apply decking on top of the ledger and joist subsystem when you determine the height of the ledger in relation to the house floor.

3. Be sure to locate and reroute if necessary all utility lines which might run in the wall where you will attach the ledger.

4. Brace the ledger against the house wall at the desired height.

5. Mark holes for lag bolts or screws on the ledger board. Typically the holes occur in pairs, one on top of the other, at the end of the ledger and then alternate in an up and down pattern. See Figure 25A. Be careful not to place your holes where you will affix joist hangers.

6. Use rustproof hot-dipped galvanized lag screws or bolts. If you are fastening the ledger to aluminum siding, use aluminum screws and washers to prevent corrosion.

7. You might want to paint the exposed cut ends of the ledger with a preservative to prevent decay.

For **wood walls**, temporarily nail once at the board's approximate center, level the board with a carpenter's level, and temporarily nail both ends. Recheck for levelness. If the ledger is level, fasten to the wall with lag screws and washers. To prevent trapping of moisture between the ledger and the exterior wall, you might want to place two or three washers over the lag screw on the back (house) side of the ledger to act as spacers.

For **stucco walls**, first drill lag screw holes into the ledger with a wood bit. Then use makeshift braces for support or enlist extra helping hands to hold the ledger in position and mark the stucco through the ledger holes with a pencil. Be certain that the ledger is level before you mark the holes on the stucco. These marked holes must be drilled with a masonry bit in order to penetrate the stucco. Once you have drilled through the stucco, you can again switch to a wood bit and then drill a slightly undersized hole (for example use a 1/4" bit for 3/8" lag screws) into the house floor frame header board.

For **masonry walls**, drill lag screw holes into the ledger with a wood bit. Then use makeshift braces for support or enlist extra helping hands to hold the ledger in position and mark the masonry through the ledger holes with a pencil. Be certain that the ledger is level before you mark the holes on the masonry. Drill with a masonry bit and create a hole wide and deep enough to accommodate an expansion shield for the lag bolt. Carefully seat the expansion shield, place the ledger board against the wall, and secure with lag bolts and washers.

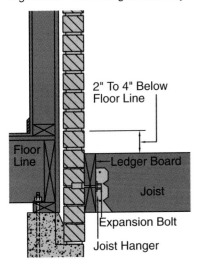

Figure 25A - Attaching to Masonry

2" To 4" Below Floor Line

Floor Line

Ledger Board

Joist

Expansion Bolt

Joist Hanger

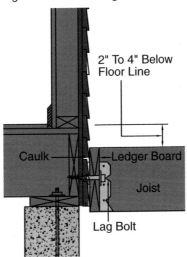

Figure 25B - Attaching to Wood

2" To 4" Below Floor Line

Caulk

Ledger Board

Joist

Lag Bolt

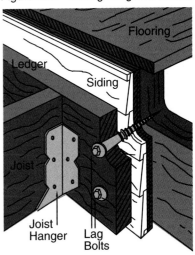

Figure 25C - Bolting Ledger to House

Flooring

Ledger

Siding

Joist

Joist Hanger

Lag Bolts

Attaching the Ledger Board to Your Home

Figure 26A - Attaching Ledger Board

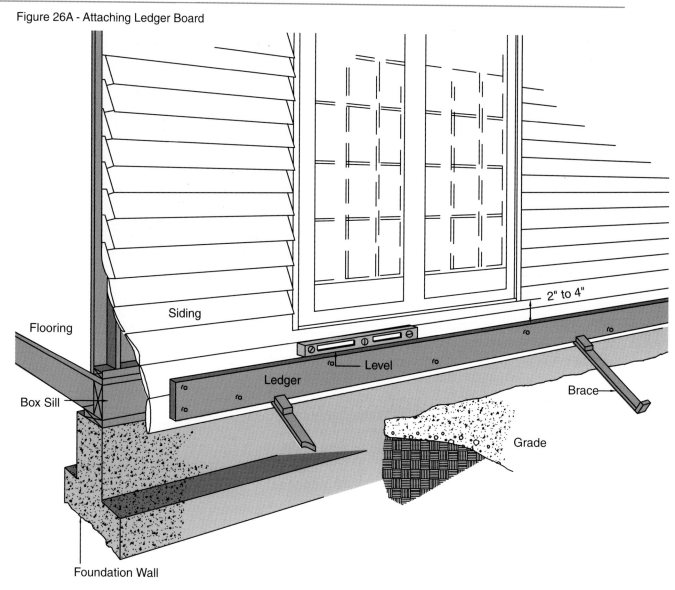

Figure 26B - Ledger Board Detail

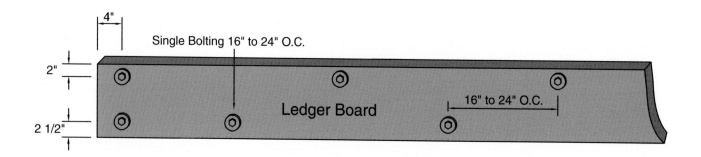

Installing Piers and Posts

First be certain you have purchased enough concrete to complete pier installation. Concrete is measured in cubic yards. To calculate the concrete required for a given number of cylindrical piers, use the following formula to find the **Total Volume in cubic yards:**

$$\textbf{Volume} = \frac{3.14 \times \text{Depth of Pier (feet)} \times \text{Diameter (feet)} \times \text{Diameter (feet)} \times \text{No. Piers}}{108}$$

Example: Concrete required for twelve 10" diameter piers, 30" deep.*

$$\textbf{Volume in cubic yards} = \frac{3.14 \times 2.5 \times .83 \times .83 \times 12}{108} = \textbf{.61 Cubic Yards}$$

*Remember to convert inches to feet (10 inches = .83 feet)   Conversion Factor: 27 Cubic Feet = 1 Cubic Yard

Figure 27A - Pier Diagrams

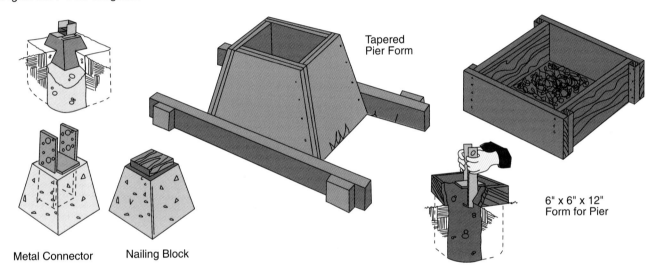

Tapered Pier Form

6" x 6" x 12" Form for Pier

Metal Connector   Nailing Block

Figure 27B - Pillars and Posts

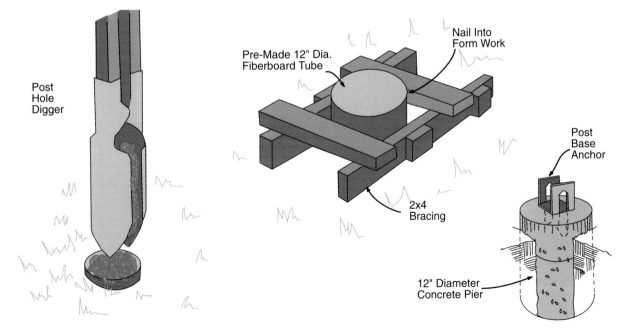

Post Hole Digger

Pre-Made 12" Dia. Fiberboard Tube

Nail Into Form Work

2x4 Bracing

Post Base Anchor

12" Diameter Concrete Pier

Installing Piers and Posts

Prepare pier forms if you are going to make poured in-place piers. Otherwise obtain precast piers with a redwood or pressure treated nailer block on top. You might want to temporarily remove pier centerline strings at this point.

1. Mix concrete according to manufacturer's instructions in a wheelbarrow or in a "half-bag" mixer. Use clean water for mixing and achieve the proper plastic consistency before you pour the concrete. If you are not using ready-mix concrete, prepare a **1:2:3 mix**—one part concrete, two parts river sand, and three parts gravel.

2. Coat the inside of the forms with oil to prevent sticking and dampen the inside of the hole with water before you pour the concrete.

3. With your post base anchors at hand, poor the concrete into the forms and tap slightly to settle. For poured in-place piers, wait for the concrete to begin to harden and set the post base anchors into the concrete. Ensure that anchors are square and level. You can drop a plumb bob from your centerline string to be certain that your anchor is centered properly. Adjust post base anchors to the correct height.

4. If you are using a precast pier, fill the pier hole with concrete up to 2"- 3" below grade level. Then spray the pier with water and then embed the pier at least 3" into the fresh concrete and twist slightly to achieve a solid bond between the concrete and the pier. Make certain that you have enough concrete in the hole so that the top of the nailer block is at least 4"-6" above grade level. Check the alignment of the pier by dropping the plumb bob from the centerline string. Finally, use a level across the nailer block and tap the pier until it is level in all directions and square.

5. Allow the concrete to harden at least 24 hours before you proceed to attach posts to piers. If you have poured your concrete during hot and dry conditions, you should cover the piers with wet burlap sacks to encourage a slow cure of the concrete.

6. If you are using precast piers and decide to secure post anchor connectors to the nailer block, wait for concrete to harden and then nail the post anchors to the nailer block with short ribbed nails.

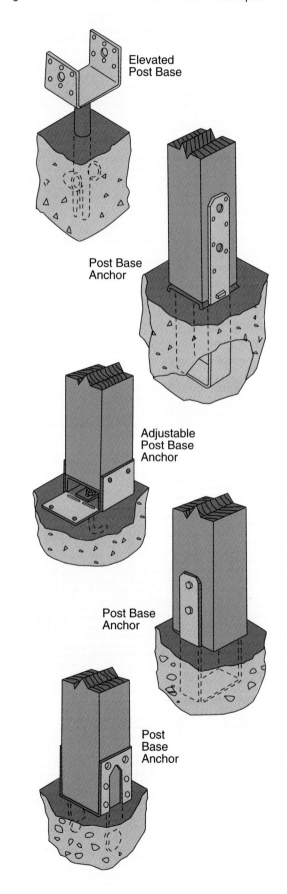

Figure 28 - Installation and Base Anchor Techniques

Elevated Post Base

Post Base Anchor

Adjustable Post Base Anchor

Post Base Anchor

Post Base Anchor

Measuring Deck Post Height

If you are building railings, some posts will extend above the deck floor to provide railing support. Follow the post bracing instructions for high-level decks but do not cut posts at the girder line.

1. Cut deck posts individually to at least 6" longer than finished post height. If you are uncertain as to the approximate finished height, drop your plumb bob from the pier centerline string and measure the distance from the string (which should be at the height of the top of the girder) to the bottom seat of post anchor connector or to the top of the nailing block. First subtract the actual height (remember that a 4x6 girder for example is only 5-1/2" high) of the girder and then add 6" to this distance to calculate your rough-in post height.

2. If your deck is a low-level deck with short posts (under 12"), simply seat the rough-in posts in the post anchor connectors, check for plumb with a level, and ensure that posts are square in the connector. Use either the pier centerline string to establish a cutting line on the post or use a string level on a line from the top of the ledger board to the post. Again you must subtract the actual (versus nominal) height of the girder from your string line to establish the cutting line on the post.

3. If your deck is a high-level deck with posts over 12", use the following instructions to ensure that posts are plumb and cut at the correct height for the girder.

4. Follow the illustration to the right and use scrap lumber to stake and support the post. First use a carpenter's level on two adjacent sides of the post to ensure that the post is plumb and then use a string level to determine the correct height of the post in relation to the ledger board. Remember that you must subtract the actual height of the girder from your stringline to establish your cutting line. Mark the cutting line with a pencil.

5. Cut marked posts at the post cutting line. Be certain that your cut through the post is a level cut.

6. Recheck your posts for plumb and either toenail (driving the nails at an angle on all four sides) the post to the pier's nailing block or seat the post in the post anchor and use short ribbed nails provided with the connector or at least 10 penny common HDG nails to connect the post to the post anchor. Nail at all the nailing holes provided in the post anchor. In earthquake prone regions, you can use lag screws to connect the post and the anchor for extra security.

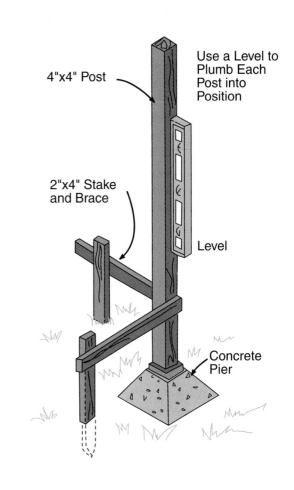

Figure 29A - Setting and Plumbing Posts

4"x4" Post

Use a Level to Plumb Each Post into Position

2"x4" Stake and Brace

Level

Concrete Pier

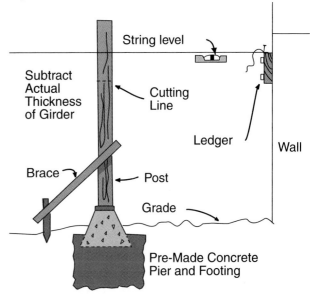

Figure 29B - Measuring Deck Post Height

String level

Subtract Actual Thickness of Girder

Cutting Line

Ledger

Wall

Brace

Post

Grade

Pre-Made Concrete Pier and Footing

Installing the Girders

Girders can be either solid or built-up from two or more 2x boards on edge. Remember that because of extra thickness 4x beams will support a greater load than built-up 2x beams. Also a 4x6 girder for example sits squarely on top of a 4x4 post (both are 3 1/2" wide) while two 2x6s spliced together (2 x 1-1/2" = 3") do not make an even connection. Whatever type of girder you select, make certain that girders are true and not badly bowed.

You might need some extra hands to lift a heavy girder into place. Use shims between girder and posts where necessary to correct for short post height and level girder before fastening to post. For the best joining of girder to post, use post cap connectors (see illustrations below for various girder to post connector options). Otherwise you can toenail girders to posts with 16 or 20 penny HDG common nails.

Figure 30 - Girder Connectors

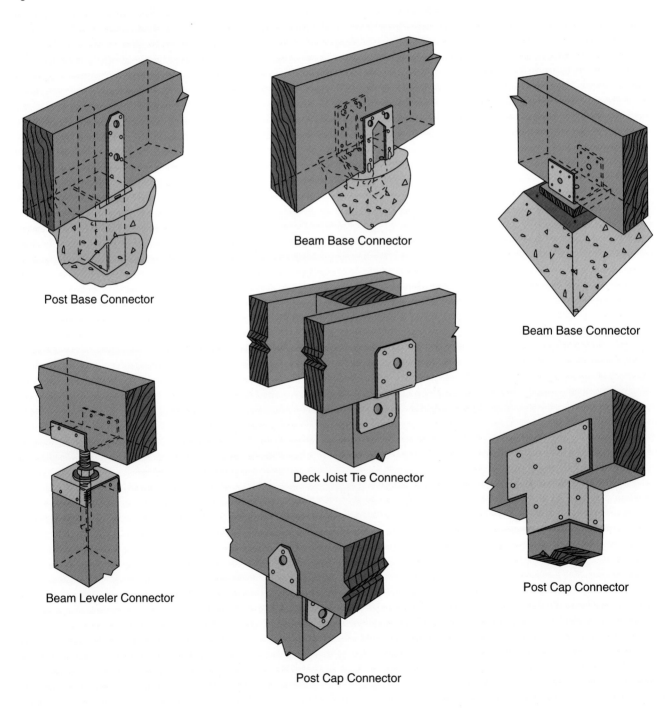

Post Base Connector

Beam Base Connector

Beam Base Connector

Beam Leveler Connector

Deck Joist Tie Connector

Post Cap Connector

Post Cap Connector

Attaching Joists and Rim Joists

1. First place rim joists (also known as perimeter or band joists) on edge at ends of ledger. Locate the joists so that the bow side of the board is facing up. Next attach rim joist to ledger with corner framing anchors or toenail to ledger board with 12 penny common nails. Be certain that rim joists run at a true right angle to your ledger.

2. Place the rim joist opposite the ledger board and use corner anchors and nails to secure the connection. Make sure that all rim joists and ledger meet at right angles and realign them if they do not.

3. Depending on the joist spacing indicated on your deck framing plan, mark the center location of joist hangers on both the ledger and the opposite rim joist. Affix joist hangers with short ribbed nails provided in accordance with the manufacturer's instructions.

4. Measure each joist individually and cut to size. Set the first joist in its hangers on the ledger board and opposite rim joist. This joist should be level on the top of the girders if you have planned correctly. Making sure that the joist is level and perpendicular, nail to both joist hangers. Follow this procedure until all joists are installed.

5. If you are using 2x8 or larger joists, you should consider installing cross blocking boards or metal cross bracing at mid-span to keep joists from flexing over spans greater than 8 feet.

6. Use **seismic/hurricane connectors** (also known as joist anchors) illustrated at the bottom of page 32 (see Figure 32C) to secure each joist as it crosses a girder. Otherwise toenail joist to beam with common nails on both sides of the joist.

Figure 31 - Basic Deck Components

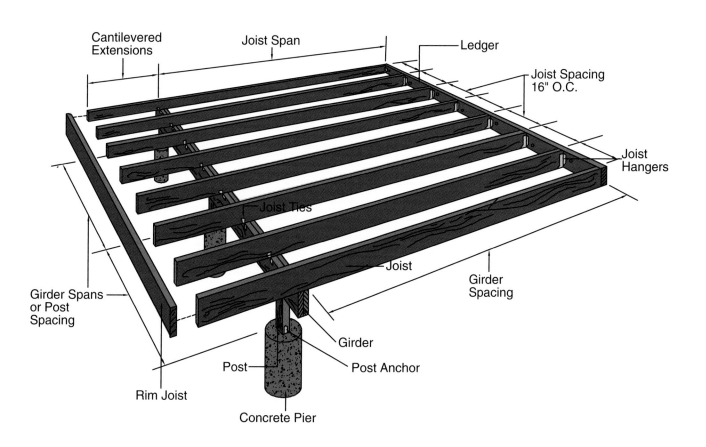

31

Attaching Joists and Rim Joists

Figure 32A - Joist Hanger

Figure 32B - Beam Frame Connector

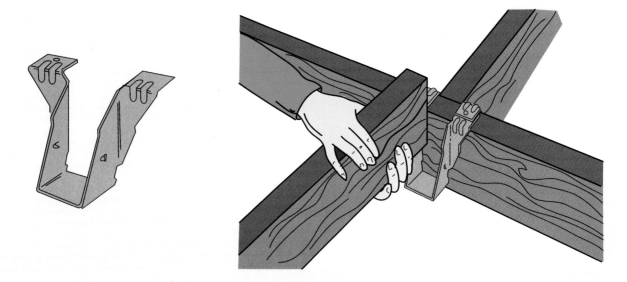

Figure 32C - Seismic/Hurricane Anchor

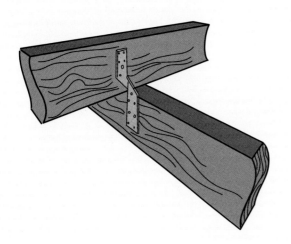

Figure 32D - Twist Strap Metal Connectors

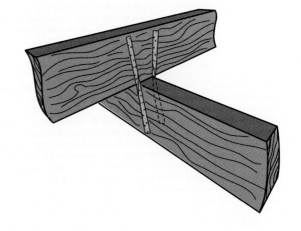

Bracing Suggestions for High Decks

Consult your local building codes for post bracing requirements for high decks. Additional factors which require post bracing are high winds, unusual deck loads like a portable spa placed on the deck surface, or earthquake activity.

Use 2x4s to brace distance less than 8 feet and 2x6s for distances greater than 8 feet.

Use at least four 3/8" x 3" lag screws and washers (two at each connection point) when you attach the brace to the post.

If you are using the **X-brace** shown at right, drill a hole where the braces intersect and secure the braces with one 3/8" x 3-1/2" lag bolt and washer.

If you construct the **Y-brace** shown below, leave approximately 1/4" gap between the two braces where they come together to ensure proper drainage. The angle where your braces meet on the post should not exceed 90 degrees.

Always cut your braces on the diagonal and cover the entire width of the post to which the brace is connected. Square cut braces detract from the appearance of your deck.

Figure 33A - X-Brace

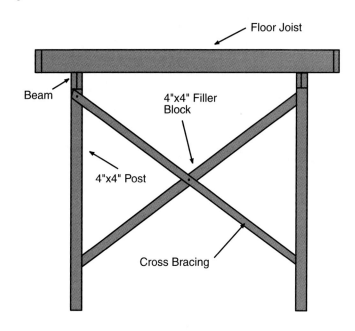

Figure 33B - Y-Brace

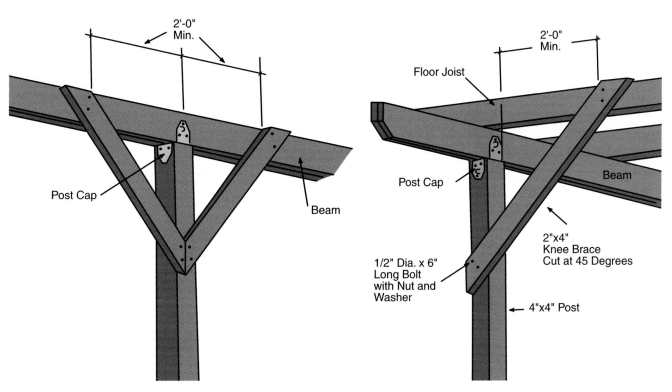

33

Stair Construction

A solid concrete stair pad is the key to successful stair construction. Don't attempt to anchor your stairs directly into the ground. Add stairs before you place surface decking.

When you have more than three steps up to your deck, you should construct a hand rail on each side of the stairs. Consult your local building code requirements.

Two stair construction methods are illustrated below-using cut stringers (upper) or the stair support method (lower). Instructions for cutting stringers are provided on page 35. The following instructions utilize the stair support method that is easier for the novice builder.

Measure the vertical height (rise) from grade to top of decking. For a 7" stair rise, divide rise dimension by 7" that will tell you how many stair risers are required. You will need two 10-1/4" metal stair supports for each stair and two 2x6 stair treads cut to a minimum 36" stair width.

Cut 2x10 or 2x12 stair stringers to size and fasten to the deck framing with a 3" corner angles and 1/4" x 1-1/2" lag screws. Use a masonry bit to drill holes for expansion shields into stair pad. Use lag screws to connect bottom corner angles to stringers and measure stringers to ensure they are parallel at top and bottom. Bolt bottom corner angles to expansion shields. Mark the step support positions on both stringers with the support below the stair tread. Use 1/4" x 1-1/2" lag screws to fasten 10-1/4" step supports to stringers and to install 2x6 stair treads.

Figure 34A - Stringers

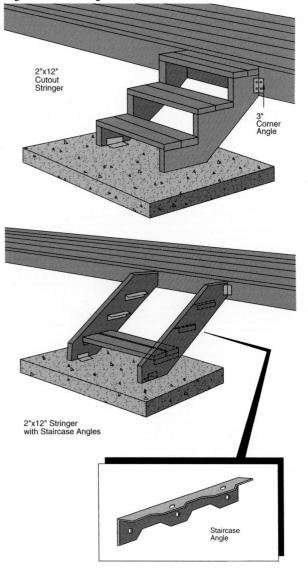

2"x12" Cutout Stringer

3" Corner Angle

2"x12" Stringer with Staircase Angles

Staircase Angle

Figure 34B - Risers

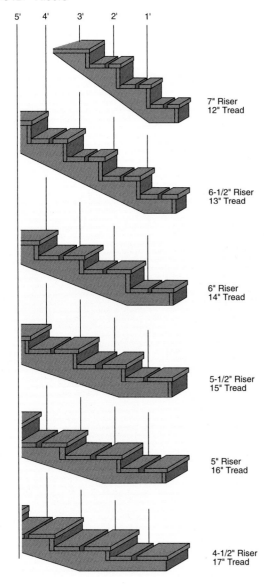

5'   4'   3'   2'   1'

7" Riser 12" Tread

6-1/2" Riser 13" Tread

6" Riser 14" Tread

5-1/2" Riser 15" Tread

5" Riser 16" Tread

4-1/2" Riser 17" Tread

Cutting Stair Stringers

If you attempt to cut your own stair stringers rather than use metal stair supports, you must select solid 2x12 material free from knots and other defects for your stringers. A stair stringer cutting template is available on page 36 to help you cut stringers.

Stringer Instructions:

1. Measure the distance from the top of the deck to the grade in inches. Divide distance by 7.25". Round off the solution to the next higher whole number. Divide the distance from the top of the porch to the grade by this whole number. The solution to the step you just completed will be your riser height.

2. Place a carpenter's square on a 2x12 as shown on page 36. Locate the 10-3/4" mark on the outside of the square's long leg. Place this mark on an edge of the 2x12. While holding this point in place, rotate the square until you can read your riser dimension on the outside edge of the short leg. Line the riser dimension up with the edge of the 2x12. Draw a line along both outside edges of the square. This marking constitutes one square and riser.

3. Slide the square along the 2x12 until you can align the 10-3/4" mark with the intersections of the edge of the board and the top of the first riser you marked. Again while holding this point in place, rotate the square until you can read your riser dimension on the outside edge of the short leg. Line the riser dimension up with the edge of the 2x12. Draw lines along both outside edges of the square. This mark outlines the second tread and riser. Repeat this process until you have drawn the required number of risers for your site condition.

4. Once all the treads and risers have been marked, move down to the line at the base of the first riser and extend that line across the 2x12. Measure 3-1/2" up from this line and draw a parallel line. This line is the actual bottom of the stringer.

Note: This 3-1/2" is a constant regardless of what you have calculated your particular riser height to be. The 3-1/2" is made up from the 1-1/2" thickness of the first tread and the 2" thickness of the concrete that is above grade.

5. Next extend the line formed by the top tread. Measure along this line 3-1/2" past the line of the top riser to locate the back of the stringer. Draw a line from this point, perpendicular to the tread, and extend to underside of stringer.

6. To lay out the notch in the underside of the stringer extend the line of the top riser to the underside of the stringer. Measure over 1-1/2" and draw a parallel line. Now take the carpenter's square and place the 1-1/2" mark from the outside edge of the square's long leg on the point where the line of the top riser intersects the underside of the stringer. Rotate the long leg of the square until it is parallel with the treads. When it is parallel, the short leg of the square will fall along the line measured 1-1/2" over from the line of the top riser. Connect the two lines with a perpendicular line drawn along the outside edge of the square's long leg.

7. Cut out the stringer on the lines that form the treads and risers, the bottom of the stringer, the back of the stringer, and the notch in the underside. Use your power saw carefully and cut each line exactly. Check the stringer by putting it in place on the rim joist and concrete pad. When one stringer has been cut correctly, you can use it as a template for the other two stringers. Again be certain that you do not cut stringers beyond the marked lines.

8. Measure for proper width between stringers at deck attachment point and attach stringers to the deck by using either a corner anchor or joist hanger. Then measure stringers at pad for proper width and mark holes for expansion shields in concrete. Drill holes with a masonry bit. Affix 5" corner anchor to concrete pad and to stringers using 1/4" x 1-1/2" lag screws and washers. Nail each stair tread with bark side up to the stringer with 12 penny hot-dipped galvanized nails or use at least 3" deck screws. You might want to predrill nail holes to prevent splitting of the stair treads.

Cutting Stair Stringers

Two Stair Support Methods

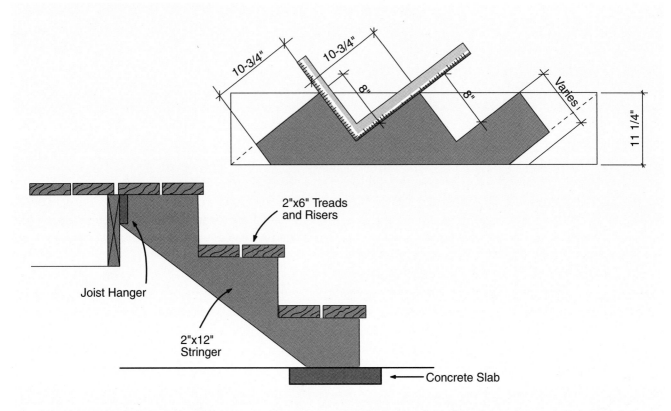

Figure 36A - Steps with Notched Stringers

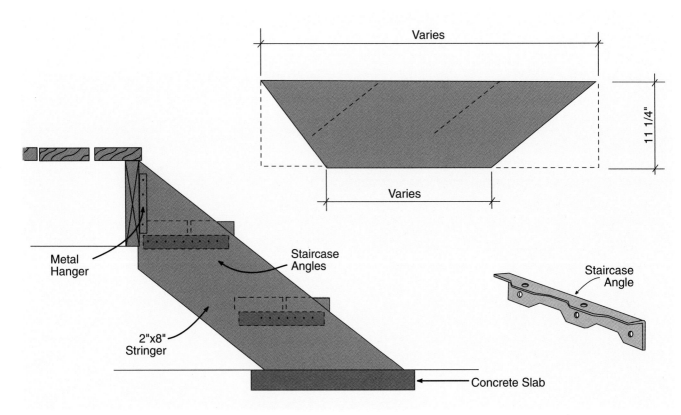

Figure 36B - Steps with Staircase Angles Holding Treads

Laying Decking

Installing decking boards provides great satisfaction as your deck nears completion. However, since the decking is the most visible part of your deck, you must proceed carefully as you nail the decking in place.

Select decking boards that are straight and free from defects. If you try to use severely warped or bowed lumber, your installation process will be tedious and you will be unhappy with the finished result.

The following instructions are for parallel decking boards laid flat and installed perpendicular to deck joists. If you are installing your decking on the diagonal, these exact instructions do not apply but the methods are similar. For diagonal decking you still start from one edge and work out from that edge until all decking is in place.

Select the straightest piece of decking for the first board and place this board at the ledger side of your deck. Place all decking boards bark or convex side up to minimize cupping and checking (see Figure 38A). The first board should be placed 3/8" from the house wall to allow for drainage.

Be sure to use only hot-dipped galvanized nails (HDG) to fasten decking.

If your budget allows, you can also consider ring shanked nails or spiral nails which are specifically designed for extra holding power. You might not want any deck nails to show – in that case investigate deck board ties that cannot be seen (see Figure 38H). Finally, you can also use 3" or longer deck screws.

Typically you will use 12 penny HDG common nails for your decking. If you predrill each nailing point, you will avoid splitting the board ends. Drive the nails at an angle (see Figure 38B). For deck screws and ring or spiral nails fasten straight down. Use three nails at board ends or joints and two at the middle joists.

Place remaining decking and be sure to measure and maintain proper 3/16" gap as you go. Set a 16 penny nail between the boards to ensure correct spacing. If your decking doesn't span the complete length of your deck, be sure to alternate the locations of decking joints. Straighten any warped boards with a chisel (see Figures 38C and 38D). When you are 6 feet from placing the last board, begin to vary spacing slightly so that you can avoid ripping a board lengthwise to fit.

When all the decking is in place, snap a chalk line along the outside face of the rim joists. Saw the deck boards at the chalk line so that they are flush with joists (see Figures 38E and 38F).

Figure 37 - Installing Decking Boards

Laying Decking

Figure 38A

Lay Boards
Bark Side
Up

Figure 38B

Drive Nails at
Opposite Angles

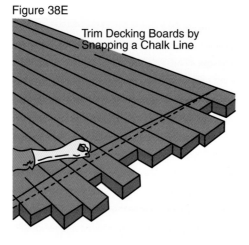

Figure 38C

Use a Wood Chisel to
Straighten Warped Boards

Figure 38D

Use a Wood Chisel to
Straighten Warped Boards

Figure 38E

Trim Decking Boards by
Snapping a Chalk Line

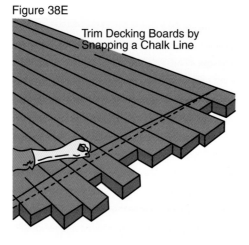

Figure 38F

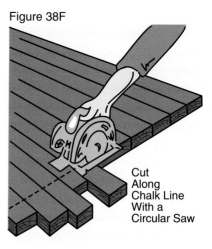

Cut
Along
Chalk Line
With a
Circular Saw

Figure 38G

Measure As You Go

One difficulty you may experience while nailing down deck boards is keeping them parallel. You can solve this problem simply by measuring the distance remaining on the joists from time to time. Take measurements along both sides and the middle as shown below. Tack a string line a foot or two away to serve as a visual guide.

If you discover that some boards are uneven as you continue your work, make your correction gradually by adjusting the space between the next three or four boards.

When you have about six feet of decking left to place, begin adjusting board spacing to avoid an unsightly gap at the end of the deck.

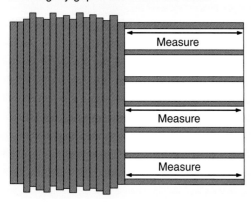

Measure

Measure

Measure

Figure 38H

Deck Board Ties For Installing Deck Boards with NO Surface Nailing

1. Deck Board Tie

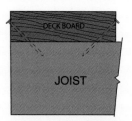

2. First Deck Board Fastened to Joist with Toenailing

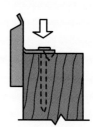

3. Locator Prongs Positions Deck Tie for Nailing on Deck Board Edge

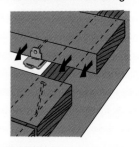

4. Slides Under Anchored Board

Fitting Decking Around Posts

If you are extending your posts to use as railing members, you will have to notch decking boards to fit around the extended posts. You must remember to support specially cut deck boards at their ends with blocking or cleat support since typically joists will not occur at all the correct positions for nailing.

Consult the illustrations below for methods of supporting decking around notched posts. Measure each side of the post allowing 3/16" on each side as a drainage gap. Use your carpenter's square to mark these measurements on the decking.

You can use either a power saw or a hand saw to make the two perpendicular cuts on your deck board. Next use a broad wood chisel to complete the notch. If you are especially handy with a power reciprocating saw, you can measure an oversize notch with arcs at the corners and use the saw to cut the entire notch in one operation.

Be sure to nail decking properly to supporting joists or cleats around the post. Use 3 nails or 2 deck screws when you fasten decking to supports around the post. Predrill nail holes so that you don't split decking boards.

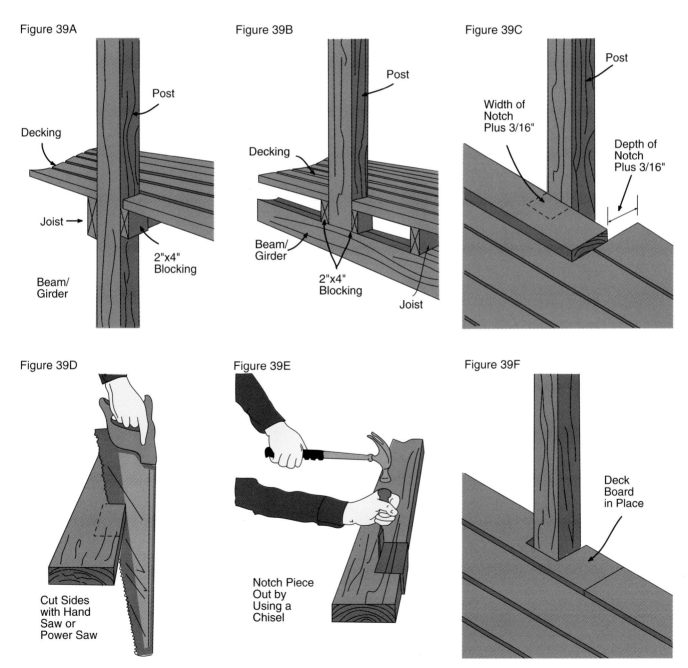

Figure 39A — Post, Decking, Joist, 2"x4" Blocking, Beam/Girder

Figure 39B — Post, Decking, Beam/Girder, 2"x4" Blocking, Joist

Figure 39C — Post, Width of Notch Plus 3/16", Depth of Notch Plus 3/16"

Figure 39D — Cut Sides with Hand Saw or Power Saw

Figure 39E — Notch Piece Out by Using a Chisel

Figure 39F — Deck Board in Place

Railing Construction

Railings require careful planning before construction begins and should not be added as an afterthought. Consult your local building department for code requirements on railing height, lateral strength, and baluster and rail spacing before you begin construction. Typical railing height is 36" from decking to the top of the cap rail.

First consider if you want to extend deck posts through the decking as major railing supports or if you want to connect 4x4 posts to the rim joists on the perimeter of the deck. See the illustrations at the right for details on these two methods of railing construction.

If you decide to use attached post construction rather than extended post construction, you must attach each post to the rim joist with at least two 3/8" x 5" lag screws and washers at the bottom of the post. For a more finished look, you might want to bevel cut the end of the 4x4 below the screw heads. Predrill the lag screw holes in the post with a 3/8" bit and don't put the holes in the beveled section of the post. Then place the post, checking for plumbness and marking the lag holes with a pencil. Drill these holes with a 1/4" bit and secure the post firmly to the rim joist with lag screws and washers.

Once your railing posts have been cut to the proper height, you will install the cap rail and other horizontal rail members. Cap rails are best constructed from either clear 2x4 or 2x6 boards laid flat. Mitre cap rails where they meet at right angles over a post as shown in the illustration at right. Use either a nailing cleat or a metal connector to make a secure connection between rail and post at points below the top of the 4x4.

Toenail rails to posts with 10 penny HDG common nails or use 3 deck screws drilled at a slant. Whatever fastener you employ, don't skimp on quality here. There's nothing more disappointing than rusting fasteners bleeding down your railings and onto your deck surface.

Balusters should be constructed from at least 2x2 material without knots that could make the baluster subject to breakage. Typical baluster spacing is 4" on center depending upon local code requirements. Be sure to keep your balusters plumb and fasten at the top and bottom with either HDG 10 penny common nails or 2-1/2" deck screws which don't require predrilling. If you have beveled the bottom of your attached rail posts, you might want to bevel the tops and bottoms of your balusters for a unified look. If the balusters do not provide the main lateral strength for the rails, you can use finishing nails instead of common nails and then sink the nail heads with a nail punch and cover the heads with an exterior wood putty.

Apply an appropriate wood finish to your completed railing, especially where the end grain of the wood is exposed on cap rails.

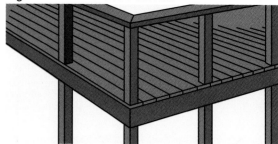

Figure 40A - Extended Post Rail

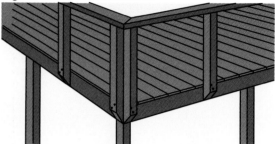

Figure 40B - Rail Post Bolted

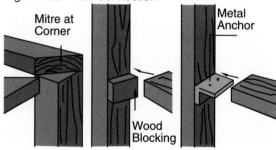

Figure 40C - Rail Connection

Mitre at Corner

Metal Anchor

Wood Blocking

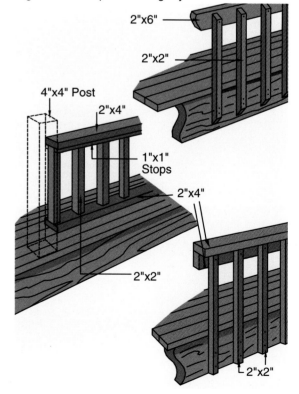

Figure 40D - Popular Railing Styles

2"x6"

2"x2"

4"x4" Post

2"x4"

1"x1" Stops

2"x4"

2"x2"

2"x2"

Bench Construction

The illustration below demonstrates one method of attached bench construction that can be added to an existing deck or built when you undertake new deck construction.

There are as many bench options as you can imagine. However, a good guideline for bench construction is that the bench seat should be at least 18" high from the decking and at least 15" deep to provide comfortable seating. A bench with an integrated backrest can be designed to serve a dual purpose on high level decks where it functions as both a seat and a railing.

No matter which bench design you select, you should use clear wood for bench seats which is free from knots, splitting, and other defects.

To construct the bench shown below, fasten two 2x6 bench supports to decking with 12 gauge 8-1/4" long bench support brackets on both sides of the bench supports. Use 1/4" x 1-1/2" lag screws and washers to connect supports to brackets and brackets to decking.

Following the dimensions shown below, cut the seat brace from 2x6 lumber. Secure the seat brace to the seat supports with 3/8" x 5-1/2" carriage bolts with nuts and washers.

Next cut three 2x6s to the correct length and place flatwise on the bench supports. Use 10 penny HDG common nails or 3" deck screws to fasten bench seat boards to bench braces. Leave 1/4" spacing between seat boards for proper drainage. Secure 2x4 trim boards at front and back of bench.

Figure 41 - Bench Construction Diagrams

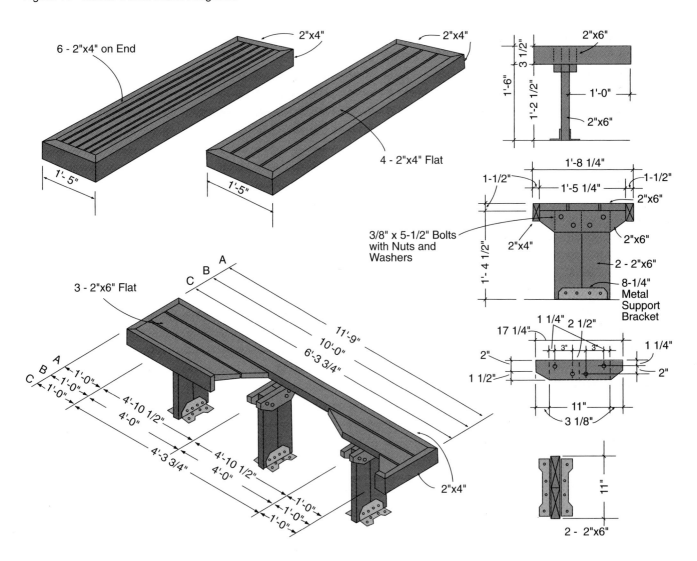

For Notes and Layout Procedures

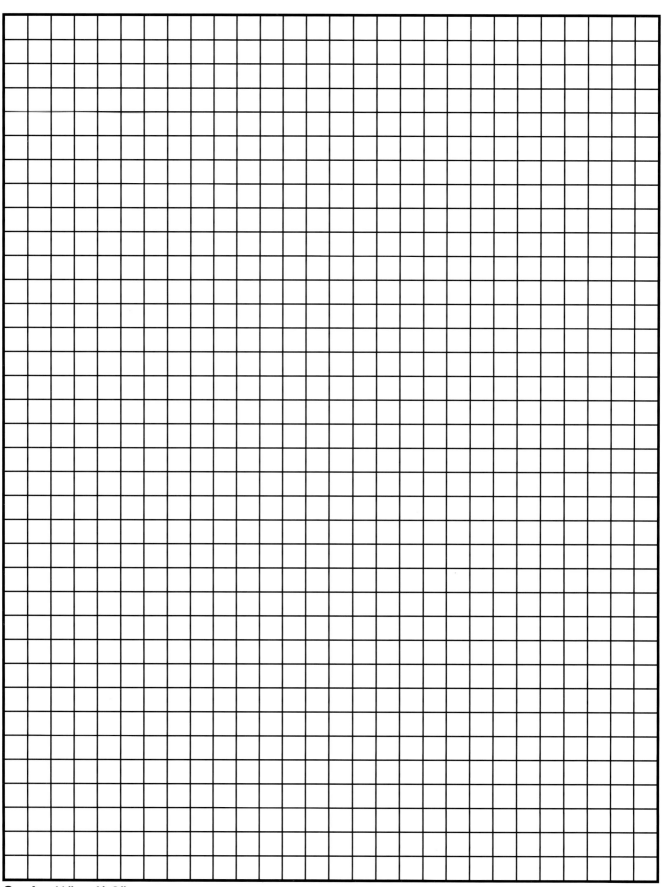

Scale: ¼" = 1'-0" per square

For Notes and Layout Procedures

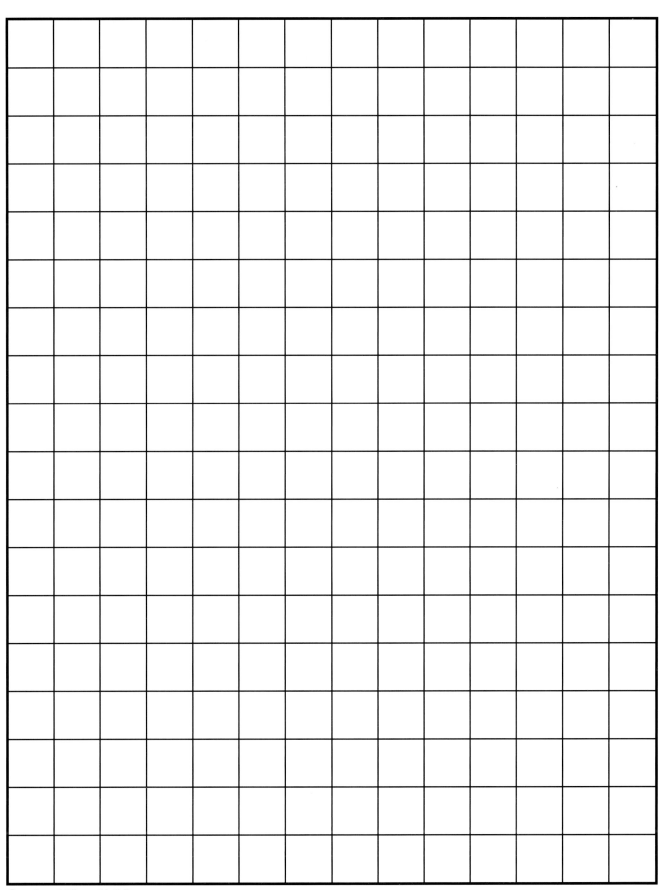

Scale: ½" = 1'-0" per square

Glossary

Anchor - Any metal connector device that is placed in wet concrete and helps to secure posts to piers.

Baluster - A vertical railing member typically cut from 2x2 stock that spans top and bottom rails.

Batterboard - Scrap lumber nailed horizontally to stakes driven near each corner of the deck excavation. Stretch nylon strings between batterboards to transfer reference points and to measure elevation.

Beam - Beams are horizontal structural members that are supported by vertical posts. Beams can support joist members on end or decking can be placed directly on beams in certain designs. Typically constructed from 2 or more 2-bys or 4-by material. See beam span chart for allowable beam spacing and spans. Also called a girder.

Blocking - Material cut from same stock as joist members and nailed between joists for horizontal stability.

Bracing - Bracing provides vertical stability to post members on high-level decks. Diagonal bracing should be lag bolted to connecting members for extra stability.

Bridging - Wood or metal cross pieces fastened between joists to provide structural strength and stability.

Cantilever - Refers to the end portion of a joist or the entire portion of the deck that extends beyond the beam.

Cap Rail - The cap rail is the topmost horizontal railing piece of deck railing. Typically 2x6 or 2x4.

Cleat - A short nailer that supports decking or stair treads.

Codes - Regulations implemented by your local building department that control the design and construction of buildings and other structures such as decks. Consult your local building department for applicable codes before you begin to build your deck.

Deck Board Tie - A metal fastener that allows you to fasten decking to joists without using nails visible on the surface of the decking. See page 38.

Deck Screws - A thin-shanked self-drilling screw that is a superior fastener for attaching decking. Especially useful in climates where decking boards must be removed and replaced due to severe weathering.

Decking - Typically 2x4, 2x6, or 5/4" radius edged lumber placed flatwise on 16" or 24" spaced joists. Decking is available in many wood species and grades. Choose your decking material carefully because decking determines the final appearance and durability of your completed deck.

Defect - Any defect in lumber whether as a result of a manufacturing imperfection or an irregularity in the timber from which the lumber was cut. Some defects are only blemishes while others can reduce strength and durability. Grading rules establish the extent and severity of wood defects.

Edge - The narrowest side of a piece of lumber that is perpendicular to both the face and the end.

Elevation - Drawing of your deck design as it will appear from the front, rear, left and right sides.

Face - The widest side of a piece of lumber that is perpendicular to both the edge and the end.

Finish - Any protective coating applied to your deck to protect against weathering. deck finishes are available as stains, paints, or preservatives.

Footing - Concrete footings help to anchor your piers in the surrounding soil and distribute weight over a larger surface area. In climates where the soil freezes, a generous footing protects against soil heaves and movement of your deck.

Frost Line - Measure of the maximum penetration of frost in the soil in a given geographic location. Depth of frost penetration varies with climate conditions.

Galvanized Nails - Hot-dipped galvanized nails (HDG) are dipped in zinc and will not rust.

Girder - Same as beam.

Grade Stamp - A stamp imprinted on dimensional lumber that identifies wood species, grade texture, moisture content, and usage. Grade descriptions such as select, finish, and common signify limiting characteristics that may occur in lumber in each grade. The stamp indicates a uniform measurement of performance that permits lumber of a given grade to be used for the same purpose, regardless of the manufacturer.

Grading - The process of excavating, leveling, and compacting the soil or gravel beneath your deck to its desired finish level. Proper grading avoids drainage problems under your completed deck.

Grain - Lumber shows either a flat or vertical grain depending on how it was cut from the log. To minimize warping along the face of the deck (known as cupping) and raising of the grain, you should place flat grain with the bark side up or facing out.

Gravel - Granular rock material that varies in size from approximately 1/4" to 3" in diameter. Results from either natural disintegration of stone or crushing and processing of rock.

Heartwood - Core of the log that resists decay.

Joist - Typically 2-by lumber which is set on edge and supports your deck. Joists in turn are supported by beams, ledgers, and rim joists. See joist span chart on page 10 for maximum allowable joist spacing and spans for a given joist size.

Joist Hanger - A metal connector available in many sizes and styles that attaches to a ledger or rim joist and makes a secure butt joint between ledger and joist.

Lag Screw - Heavy-duty fastener with hexagonal bolt head that provides extra fastening power for railing posts, ledgers, and other critical structural connections. Use galvanized lag screws and washers to prevent rust.

Ledger - The ledger board is attached with lag screws to the side of your house in deck construction. The ledger supports joists that are attached to the ledger with joist hangers.

Live Load - The predetermined load that a deck is capable of supporting expressed in pounds per square foot. Live load includes moving and variable loads such as people, furniture, or portable spas.

Metal Connectors - Used to augment of replace nails as fasteners, metal connectors are critical for lasting and sturdy deck construction.

Glossary

Moisture Content - Moisture content of wood is the weight of water in wood expressed as a percentage of the weight of wood from which all water has been removed. The drier the lumber the less the lumber will shrink and warp on your finished deck. Surfaced lumber with a moisture content of 19% results in a "S-GRN" stamp to indicate surfaced green. Avoid green lumber especially when selecting your boards.

Pea Gravel - Approximately 1/4" round gravel material which can be used in a 4"-6" layer to cover the soil under your deck. Provides drainage and prevents soil-to-wood contact for decks built on sleepers rather than piers.

Perimeter - Outside boundary of the deck structure.

Perpendicular - At a 90 degree or right angle.

Pier - Piers support the total weight load of your deck and anchor the deck to the soil. Concrete piers can either be precast in a pyramidal shape with a nailing block on top or poured in place. Precast piers are typically used in climates where the soil does not freeze hard. Poured in place piers are utilized where the soil freezes and must extend a certain depth below the frost line. Either precast or poured in place piers should have adequate footings to prevent movement of the pier in the soil. Consult your local building department for requirements regarding pier type and placement.

Pilot Hole - A slightly undersized hole drilled in lumber that prevents splitting of the wood when nailed.

Plumb - Absolutely vertical. Determined with either a plumb bob or spirit level.

Post - The vertical support that bears the weight of the joists and attached decking. Typically posts are at least 4x4 lumber. When post height exceeds a limit defined by your local building code, posts must be stabilized by bracing. Vertical railing supports are also known as posts.

Pressure-treated - Refers to the process of forcing preservative compounds into the fiber of the wood. Handle pressure-treated lumber with caution and do not inhale or burn its sawdust. Certain types of pressure-treated lumber are suitable for ground contact use while others must be used above ground. While more expensive than untreated lumber, pressure-treated wood resists decay and is recommended where naturally decay-resistant species like cedar or redwood are unavailable or too costly.

Rail - Any horizontal railing member.

Redwood - Decay-resistant and stable wood for long-lasting deck construction. Redwood grades from best to worst are: Clear All Heart (no knots), Construction Heart (small knots), construction Common (sapwood), Merchantable Heart (knots and knotholes), and Merchantable (sapwood with knots and knotholes). Heart grades provide the greatest decay resistance.

Reinforcing Bar - A steel rod that provides internal reinforcement for concrete piers. Also known as rebar.

Right Triangle, 3-4-5 - A means of ensuring squareness when you lay out your deck. Mark a vertical line at exactly 4'-0" from the angle you want to square. Then mark a horizontal line at exactly 3'-0" from the crossing vertical line. Measure the distance diagonally between both the 3' and 4' marks and when the distance measures exactly 5'-0" you have squared a 90 degree angle between lines.

Rim Joist - A perimeter joist to which the deck joists are attached.

Rise - Refers to the vertical height between each step in stair construction.

Sapwood - Outer layers of growth between the bark and heartwood. Less decay-resistant than heartwood.

Scale - A system of representation in plan drawing where small dimensions represent an equivalent large dimension. In typical deck plans the drawings are said to be scaled down. Scale is expressed as an equation such as 1/4"=1'-0"

Sleeper - Typically a decay-resistant 4x4 member which is placed horizontally on the ground or gravel bed and which supports decking. Recommended use is only in dry climates with stable soil.

Slope - A measurement of ground inclination and expressed as a percentage of units of vertical rise per 100 units of horizontal distance.

Spacing - In deck construction the distance between joist members and measured from center to center.

Span - The distance between beam supports which is measured center to center.

Spirit Level - A sealed cylinder with a transparent tube nearly filled with liquid forming a bubble used to indicate true vertical and horizontal alignment when the bubble is centered in the length of the tube.

Stair Stringer - An inclined 2-by member that supports the treads of a stair. Stringers can be notched with a template pattern or unnotched where treads are supported with metal step support brackets. Also known as carriage or riser.

Step Support - Step supports are 10 1/4" or 8 1/4" long specially configured brackets made from 12 gauge galvanized structural grade steel. They make it easier to build stairs when it is necessary to adjust the angle of the stringers to span the distance between the deck and the ground.

String Level - A spirit level mounted in a frame with prongs at either end for hanging on a string. Determines level across string lines.

Texture - Refers to the surface finish of lumber.

Tread - Treads provide the horizontal stepping surface in stair construction. To ensure against tread breakage, use clear 2-by wood without knots for treads.

Trim Board - A nonstructural board that covers the end of deck boards or is abutted to the rim joist. To prevent warping, you can attach trim boards with screws.

Toenail - To drive a nail at an angle. When you toenail a post to a beam for example, you should drive the nail so that one-half the nail is in each member.

Zinc-coated - Refers to fasteners coated with zinc, a non-corrosive metal used as a galvanizing material.

Ready to Start Some Serious Planning?

Now that you have read this do-it-yourself manual, you're ready to start serious planning. As you can see, there are many details to consider, and they all tie together for successful completion of your project.

If the procedures appear at first confusing, reread the information outlined in this book several times before deciding which phases of construction you want to handle yourself and which might require professional assistance.

Because drawing up your own plan from scratch can be time consuming and difficult for the inexperienced builder, you might want to make planning and cost estimating easier by selecting a design from those shown in this book.

If blueprints with lumber lists are not immediately available from your building material dealer, you can order them by using the order form in the back of this book. If after reviewing the blueprints you still have questions, talk them over with your lumber dealer. Most dealers are familiar with construction and will be glad to help you.

The following pages include an assortment of deck plans and deck-related plans. Remember that construction blueprints can be obtained by using the order form on page 80. All blueprint plans include a complete material list, exterior elevations, sections, details and instructions for the successful completion of your project.

Example of a Typical Project Plan Sheet

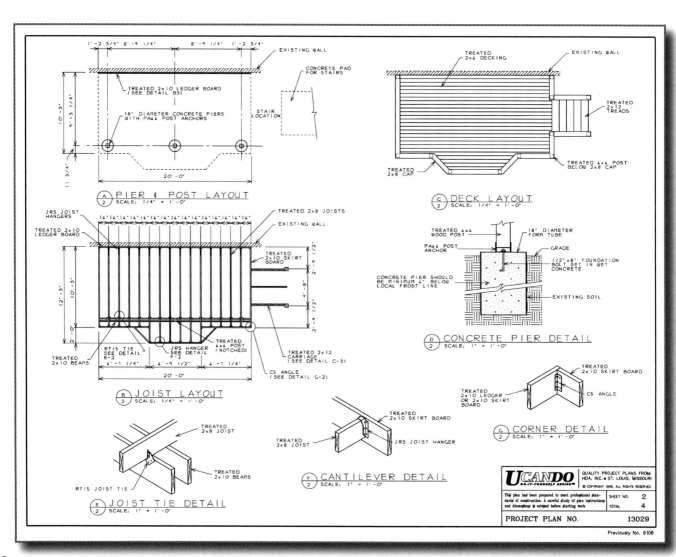

Project Plans
Decks, Gazebos, Benches and MORE

Two-Level Raised Deck

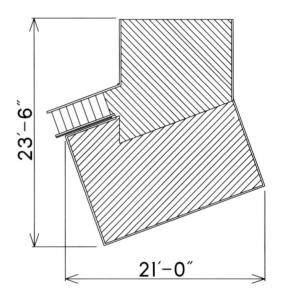

23'-6"
21'-0"

- Overall size - 21'-0" x 23'-6"
  - lower deck - 18'-0" x 12'-0"
  - upper deck - 12'-0" x 12'-9"
- Can be built at any height
- Adaptable to any lot situation
- Complete list of materials
- Step-by-step instructions

Deck with Multiple Levels

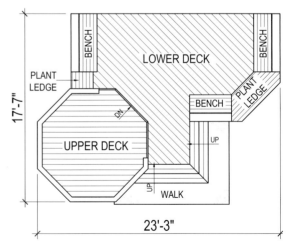

BENCH — LOWER DECK — BENCH
PLANT LEDGE
17'-7"
BENCH
PLANT LEDGE
DN
UPPER DECK
UP
UP — WALK
23'-3"

- Size - 23'-3" x 17'-7"
- Plenty of space is offered for grand outdoor living
- Built-in benches and a plant ledge provide beauty and function
- Complete list of materials
- Step-by-step instructions

Plan #DM2-002D-3023

Price Code P5

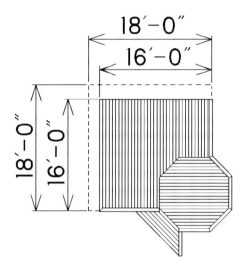

Deck with Sunken Area

- Two popular sizes -
  16' x 16'
  18' x 18'
- Unique sunken area adds interest to this deck
- Perfect addition to enhance outdoor entertaining
- Complete list of materials
- Step-by-step instructions

Plan #DM2-002D-3027

Price Code P4

Bay Deck with Railing

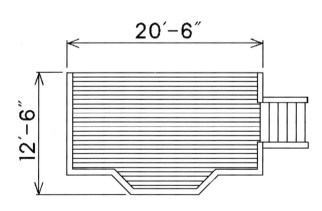

- Size - 20'-6" x 12'-6"
- Adds beauty and value to your home
- Unique layout with built-in bay
- Complete list of materials
- Step-by-step instructions

To order online visit www.projectplans.com

Plan #DM2-002D-3004

Price Code P3

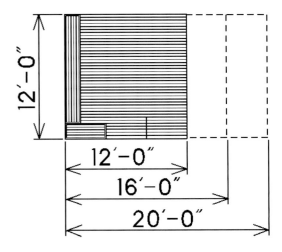

Low Patio Decks

- Three popular sizes -
    12' x 12'
    16' x 12'
    20' x 12'
- Built-in seating
- Perfect for entertaining
- Complete list of materials
- Step-by-step instructions

Plan #DM2-107D-3002

Price Code P4

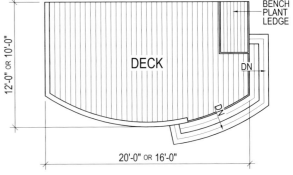

Low-Level Deck

- Sizes -
    20' x 12'
    20' x 10'
    16' x 12'
    16' x 10'
- Enjoy the outdoors with this beautiful backyard addition
- Complete list of materials
- Step-by-step instructions

Plan #DM2-002D-3002

Price Code P4

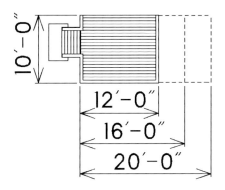

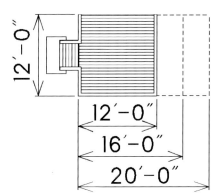

Expandable Decks

- Six popular sizes -
    - 12' x 10'   12' x 12'
    - 16' x 10'   16' x 12'
    - 20' x 10'   20' x 12'
- Functional decks in a variety of sizes to fit your every need
- Complete list of materials
- Step-by-step instructions

Plan #DM2-002D-3021

Price Code P4

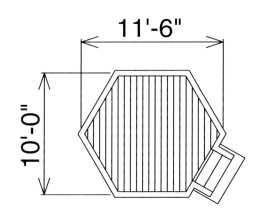

Hexagon Deck

- Size - 11'-6" x 10'-0"
- Free-standing design
- Attractive deck with a choice of two railing styles
- Simple construction - easy to build
- Complete list of materials
- Step-by-step instructions

To order online visit www.projectplans.com

Raised Patio Decks

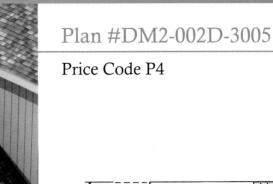

Plan #DM2-002D-3005

Price Code P4

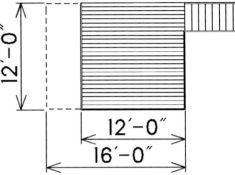

- Two popular sizes -
    12' x 12'
    16' x 12'
- Both decks can be constructed at any height
- Can be built to fit any lot situation
- Complete list of materials
- Step-by-step instructions

Easy Decks

Plan #DM2-002D-3011

Price Code P3

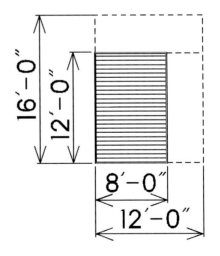

- Three great sizes -
    8' x 12'
    12' x 12'
    12' x 16'
- Low cost construction
- Can be built with standard lumber
- Adaptable to all grades
- Complete list of materials
- Step-by-step instructions

Plan #DM2-002D-3016

Price Code P5

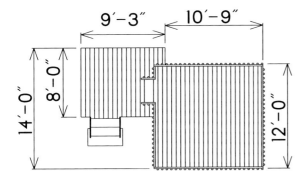

Split-Level Deck

- Overall size - 20' x 14'
    - lower deck - 9' x 8'
    - upper deck - 12' x 12'
- Can be built with standard lumber
- Adaptable to all grades
- Complete list of materials
- Step-by-step instructions

Plan #DM2-002D-3019

Price Code P5

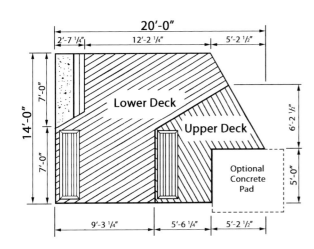

Two-Level Spa Deck

- Overall size - 20'-0" x 14'-0"
    - lower deck - 14'-9" x 14'-0"
    - upper deck - 10'-8 3/4" x 11'-2 1/2"
- Designed for self-contained portable spas
- Free-standing or next to house
- Complete list of materials
- Step-by-step instructions

To order online visit www.projectplans.com

Two-Level Deck with Bench

- Overall size - 14' x 15'
    lower deck - 8' x 8'
    upper deck - 12' x 9'
- Unique, attractive design features two-level deck and bench
- Adds great value to your home
- Complete list of materials
- Step-by-step instructions

Plan #DM2-002D-3007

Price Code P5

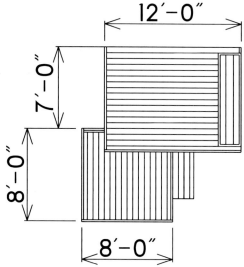

Plan #DM2-002D-3010

Price Code P5

High-Low Deck

- Overall size - 19' x 24'
    lower deck size - 15'-5 1/2" x 12'-11"
    upper deck size - 10'-0" x 8'-0"
- Designed as an add-on to an existing deck or as a complete unit
- Benches can be arranged as needed
- Features a unique conversation area or optional fire pit
- Complete list of materials
- Step-by-step instructions

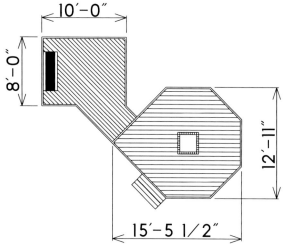

To order online visit www.projectplans.com

Plan #DM2-002D-3009

Price Code P4

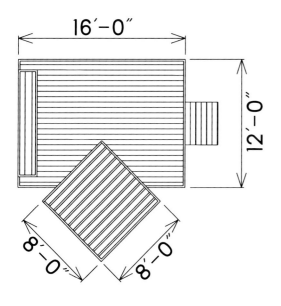

Two-Level Garden Deck

- Overall size - 16' x 19'
  main deck - 16' x 12'
  upper deck - 8' x 8'
- Unique design features decorative plant display area or sundeck
- Built-in seating
- Can be free-standing or attached
- Complete list of materials
- Step-by-step instructions

Plan #DM2-002D-3006

Price Code P4

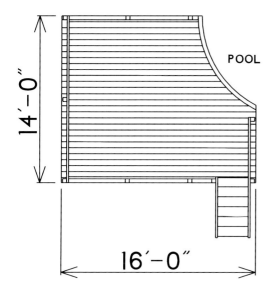

POOL

Pool Deck

- Size - 16' x 14'
- Can be built to fit any size pool
- Simple but sturdy design with built-in gate
- Makes cleaning and maintaining the pool a breeze
- Complete list of materials
- Step-by-step instructions

Plan #DM2-064D-3003

Price Code P5

Contemporary Curved Deck

- Sizes -
  - 24' x 14'
  - 26' x 14'
  - 28' x 14'
- Curved design adapts to any home
- Bench details included
- Complete list of materials
- Step-by-step instructions

For decks, fences and siding, penetrating finishes are superior to coatings such as varnish or polyurethane because they do not crack, peel or become opaque.

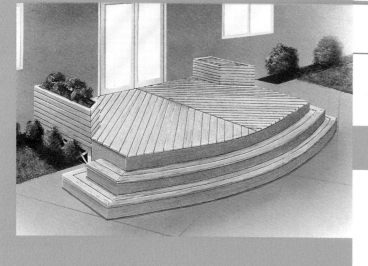

Plan #DM2-064D-3002

Price Code P5

Casual Curved Deck

- Sizes -
  - 16' x 8'
  - 16' x 10'
  - 16' x 12'
  - 20' x 12'
- Planter and bench details included
- Complete list of materials
- Step-by-step instructions

Even though your local codes may not have requirements for the spacing of balusters, try to keep them 4-inches apart on center so a small child cannot fall through.

Plan #DM2-064D-3005

Price Code P4

Angular Low-Level Deck

- Sizes -
    - 20' x 14'
    - 24' x 18'
    - 28' x 22'
- Angular design is ideal for a home with elegant lines on a flat lot
- Complete list of materials
- Step-by-step instructions

A trellis roof can be added to your deck to help shade the sun if you have a particularly sunny spot chosen for your deck location.

Plan #DM2-064D-3004

Price Code P3

Octagon Sun Deck

- Sizes -
    - 9' diameter
    - 12' diameter
    - 16' diameter
- Easy to build deck makes a great hot tub platform or free-standing sun deck
- Complete list of materials
- Step-by-step instructions

Keep in mind, a north-side deck will probably be the coolest location. Southern or Western orientations may be very warm in the middle of summer unless you have an overhead screen or shade tree.

To order online visit www.projectplans.com

Plan #DM2-064D-3006

Price Code P4

Mid-Level Deck

- Sizes -
    14' x 10'
    16' x 12'
    20' x 12'
- Charming deck fits any home style
- Bench and planter details included
- Complete list of materials
- Step-by-step instructions

If you think your dream deck is too large for your house, break up the expanse by building smaller sections on multiple levels.

Plan #DM2-064D-3007

Price Code P4

Split-Level Deck

- Sizes -
    12' x 14'
    16' x 14'
    20' x 14'
- Cantilevered deck can be easily adapted for any height
- Complete list of materials
- Step-by-step instructions

If possible, size your deck in 2-foot or 4-foot increments. You'll have to buy standard lumber lengths anyway, and there's no point in wasting that material when you could have a larger deck for the same amount of money.

Plan #DM2-064D-3009

Price Code P6

Multi-Level Deck with Spa

- Lower deck size - 27' x 20'-6"
- Upper deck size - 18' x 10'
- Perfectly designed getaway for backyard relaxation and recreation
- Complete list of materials
- Step-by-step instructions

Before winter arrives sweep away all leaves, pine needles and branches from your deck. When dirt and leaves build up they cause standing water or other moisture to stay on top of the deck rather than drain through.

Plan #DM2-064D-3008

Price Code P6

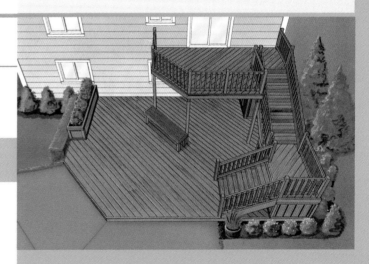

Custom Split-Level Deck

- Lower deck size -
    22' x 16'
    24' x 16'
    26' x 16'
- Upper deck size -
    12' x 8'
- Spacious deck can accommodate the needs of today's active lifestyle
- Complete list of materials
- Step-by-step instructions

Consider adding a trellis, pergola, or other outdoor structure to your deck. Spark your ideas by visiting your local home center for ideas on these enhancements and other gardening ideas.

Plan #DM2-002D-3001

Price Code P6

Deck with Gazebo

- Size - 24'-0" x 15'-6"
- Height floor to peak - 12'-2"
- Perfect for outdoor entertaining
- Gazebo adds unique flair to this deck
- Complete list of materials
- Step-by-step instructions

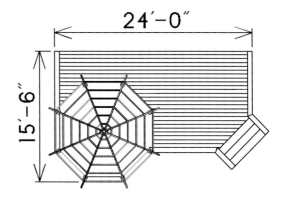

Plan #DM2-002D-3029

Price Code P6

Tiered Deck with Gazebo

- Overall size - 28'-6" x 22'-6 1/2"
    Deck "A" - 9'-0" x 15'-6"
    Deck "B" - 6'-6" x 8'-6"
    Deck "C" - 14'-0" x 12'-0"
    Gazebo "D" - 9'-6" x 8'-3" sided
    Walkway "E" - 3'-0" x 7'-0"
- Gazebo offers privacy and shade
- Build complete or add on later
- Complete list of materials
- Step-by-step instructions

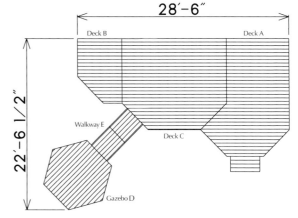

Plan #DM2-002D-3026

Price Code P5

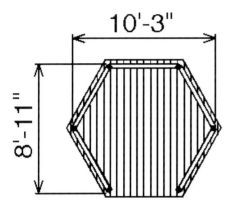

Six-Sided Gazebo

- Size - 10'-3" x 8'-11"
- Height from top of floor to peak - 10'-9"
- Ideal for small gatherings
- This traditional design will enhance any outdoor setting
- Complete list of materials
- Step-by-step instructions

Plan #DM2-063D-3002

Price Code P6

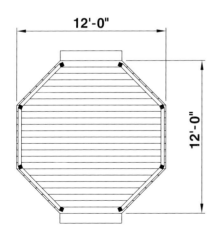

Eight-Sided Victorian Gazebo

- Size - 12' x 12'
- Building height - 17'
- Victorian accents create a charming feel
- Elegant weather vane enhances the structure
- Provides a wonderful place for outdoor entertaining
- Complete list of materials
- Plans are printed on 8 1/2" x 11" pages

Six-Sided Gazebo

- Size - 8'-3" x 9'-6"
- Height floor to peak - 12'-10"
- Complements any setting
- Cozy gazebo is great for entertaining a small group
- Complete list of materials
- Step-by-step instructions

Plan #DM2-002D-3018

Price Code P5

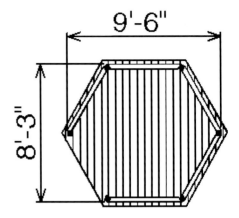

Plan #DM2-063D-3004

Price Code P6

Square Gazebo

- Size - 12' x 12'
- Building height - 16'-6"
- Roof pitch - 12/12
- Provides a wonderful place for outdoor entertainment
- Complete list of materials
- Plans are printed on 8 1/2" x 11" pages

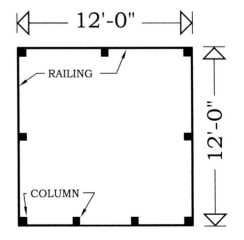

To order online visit www.projectplans.com

Plan #DM2-063D-3003

Price Code P6

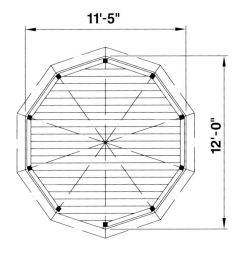

11'-5"

12'-0"

Ten-Sided Gazebo

- Size - 11'-5" x 12'-0"
- Building height - 16'
- Unique gazebo that is easy to build
- Complete list of materials
- Plans are printed on 8 1/2" x 11" pages

Plan #DM2-063D-3000

Price Code P6

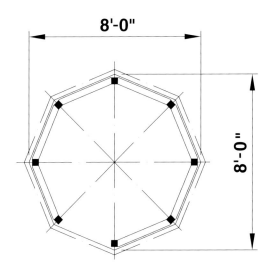

8'-0"

8'-0"

Eight-Sided Gazebo

- Size - 8' x 8'
- Building height - 13'
- Graceful accents makes this gazebo one-of-a-kind
- Complete list of materials
- Plans come printed on 8 1/2" x 11" pages

To order online visit www.projectplans.com

Octagon Gazebo

Plan #DM2-002D-3000

Price Code P6

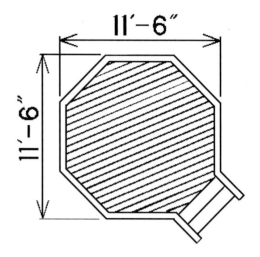

- Size - 11'-6" x 11'-6"
- Height floor to peak - 14'-7"
- Large gazebo has plenty of space for outdoor entertaining
- This attractive structure will complement any setting
- Complete list of materials
- Step-by-step instructions

Arbor / Bench

Plan #DM2-063D-3001

Price Code P4

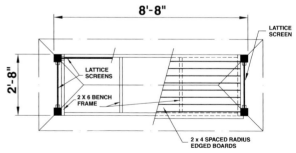

- Size - 8'-8" x 2'-8"
- Building height - 10'-4"
- Attractive enclosing lattice screens
- Roof provides shelter from the elements
- Complete list of materials
- Plans are printed on 8 1/2" x 11" pages

To order online visit www.projectplans.com

Plan #DM2-064D-3001

Price Code P6

Nostalgic Gazebo

- Sizes -
    - 9' diameter
    - 12' diameter
    - 16' diameter
- Elegant design adapts to multi-seasonal use
- Lattice details add style and character to this popular gazebo
- Complete list of materials
- Step-by-step instructions

To maintain the natural look of the wood you've chosen when building, you should apply a sealer as soon as your gazebo is constructed. For a more rustic look, wait and apply the sealer once the wood has weathered.

Plan #DM2-064D-3000

Price Code P6

Garden Gazebo

- Sizes -
    - 10' x 10'
    - 12' x 12'
    - 16' x 16'
- A picturesque backyard getaway
- This unique garden gazebo uses glass panels and wooden doors to create a style unlike any other
- Complete list of materials
- Step-by-step instructions

If you are building with cedar, use a clear water repellent sealer after construction has been completed. This will maintain the beauty and color of the wood. Applications should be made every two to four years.

To order online visit www.projectplans.com

Patio Covers

Plan #DM2-002D-3014

Price Code P4

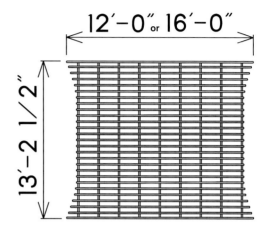

- Two sizes -
  12' x 13'-2 1/2"
  16' x 13'-2 1/2"
- Designed to cover an existing deck or patio or used as a pavilion
- Can be built with standard lumber
- Plan includes an alternate bench design
- Complete list of materials
- Step-by-step instructions

Four-Sided Gazebo

Plan #DM2-002D-3025

Price Code P5

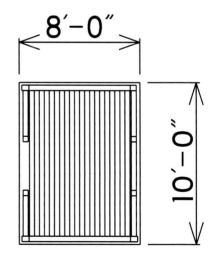

- Size - 8' x 10'
- Height from top of floor to peak - 11'
- Gable roof construction
- A unique and functional addition to your yard
- Adds additional shade and privacy for outdoor entertaining
- Complete list of materials
- Step-by-step instructions

Plan #DM2-002D-3008

Price Code P5

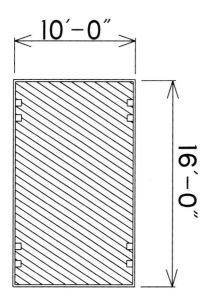

10'-0"

16'-0"

Shaded Deck

- Size - 16'-0" x 10'-0" x 9'-6" high
- Deck design has a sun-screen covering
- Enhance your outdoors with this shaded deck
- Complete list of materials
- Step-by-step instructions

Plan #DM2-102D-3000

Price Code P6

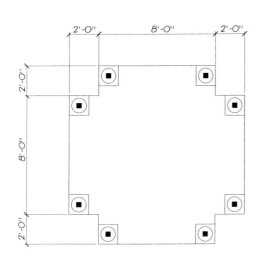

2'-0" 8'-0" 2'-0"

2'-0"

8'-0"

2'-0"

Pergola

- Size - 12' x 12'
- Creates a wonderful shaded outdoor area for dining or entertaining
- Attractive columns add a touch of distinction
- Complete list of materials

Easy Patio Cover

Plan #DM2-002D-3015

Price Code P4

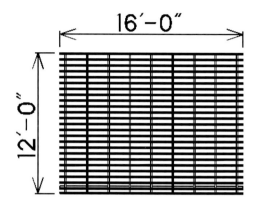

16'-0"

12'-0"

- Size - 16' x 12'
- Attractive patio cover features a sun-screen covering
- Add value and beauty to your home
- Complete list of materials
- Step-by-step instructions

Garden Entryway

Plan #DM2-002D-3017

Price Code P5

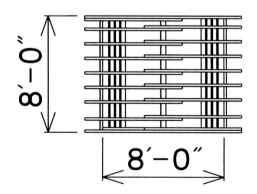

8'-0"

8'-0"

- Size - 8' x 8'
- Height peak to grade - 10'-10"
- Unique, attractive design that will complement either your garden or home
- Simple construction
- Complete list of materials
- Step-by-step instructions

Plan #DM2-002D-3012

Price Code P3

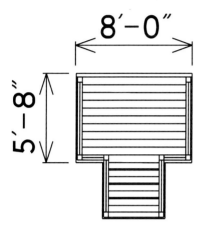

Entry Porches

- Size - 8'-0" x 5'-8"
- Two popular styles - contemporary and colonial
- Attractive designs to fit any type of home
- Can be free-standing or attached
- Adaptable for trailer or home use
- Complete list of materials
- Step-by-step instructions

Plan #DM2-002D-3024

Price Code P4

Patio Covers - Roof / Sun Shade

- Patio roof size - 16' x 9'
- Sun shade size - 20' x 10'
- A unique and functional addition to your home
- Complete list of materials
- Step-by-step instructions

To order online visit www.projectplans.com

3 Bridges

- Three styles and sizes -
  Plan 1 - 18'-0" x 4'-11"
  Plan 2 - 13'-5" x 4'-11"
  Plan 3 - 11'-0" x 4'-11"
- Enhance your outdoors
- Complete list of materials
- Step-by-step instructions

Plan #DM2-002D-3003

Price Code P5

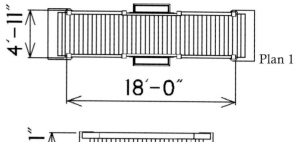

Plan 1

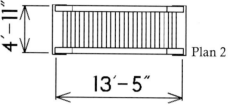

Plan 2

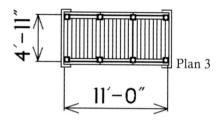

Plan 3

Entry Porches

- Two popular styles -
  Plan 1 - 6'-5" x 5'-5"
  Plan 2 - 7'-5" x 6'-5"
- Functional porches that enhance any entrance
- Complete list of materials
- Step-by-step instructions

Plan #DM2-002D-3028

Price Code P3

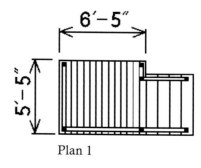

Plan 1

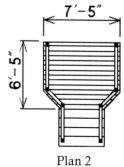

Plan 2

Plan #DM2-002D-3022

Price Code P3

Deck Railings

- Six styles to choose from
- Can easily be added to your existing deck
- Complement any design
- Easily adaptable to any outdoor structure
- Complete list of materials
- Step-by-step instructions

Plan #DM2-002D-3013

Price Code P4

Deck Enhancements

- Four unique designs -
    Planter box - 2'-0" x 2'-0"
    Decorative screen - 7'-0" x 5'-6"
    Bench - 6'-0" x 1'-8"
    End table - 2'-6" x 1'-5"
- Adds to any existing deck
- Can be free-standing or attached to your deck
- Complete list of materials
- Step-by-step instructions

Plan #DM2-002D-0013

Price Code P3

Leisure Bench with Table

- Bench size - 60" x 20" x 36" high
- Table size - 48" x 20" x 18" high
- Enhance your garden, patio or deck
- Complements any outdoor setting
- Complete list of materials
- Step-by-step instructions

Plan #DM2-066D-0019

Price Code P3

Planter Bench

- Bench size - 36" long x 15" wide
- Planter boxes size - 20 1/2" square x 17" tall
- Modular construction allows builder to configure as preferred
- Complete list of materials
- Step-by-step instructions

Plan #DM2-066D-0021

Price Code P3

Porch Swing

- Size - 60" long as pictured, but length may be adjusted
- A handsome and comfortable addition to any porch or patio
- Complete list of materials
- Step-by-step instructions

Plan #DM2-066D-0006

Price Code P3

Canopy Glider Swing

- Size - 8'-0" x 6'-5" x 8'-0" high
- Seats four adults
- Includes small table with cut-outs for drinks
- Complete list of materials
- Step-by-step instructions
- Full-size traceable patterns

Plan #DM2-066D-0020

Price Code P3

Porch Rocker

- Size - 42" tall x 24 1/2" wide x 28" deep
- Made from standard redwood lumber
- Features mostly straight cuts with full-size patterns for the curved cuts
- Complete list of materials
- Step-by-step instructions

Plan #DM2-066D-0023

Price Code P3

Adirondack Quartet

- Four easy-to-build Adirondack projects
- Complete list of materials
- Step-by-step instructions

To order online visit www.projectplans.com

Plan #DM2-002D-0012

Price Code P3

Garden Swing with Canopy

- Canopy size - 12'-0" x 5'-0" x 7'-6" high
- Bench size - 6'-0" long
- Attractive design features a sun-screen canopy
- Perfect for enjoying the outdoors in style
- Complete list of materials
- Step-by-step instructions

Plan #DM2-066D-0018

Price Code P3

Octagon Table Set

- Size - table measures 55" across x 30" tall
- Seats eight or more on combination of two-seat benches and single-seat stools
- Complete list of materials
- Step-by-step instructions

Plan #DM2-066D-0022

Price Code P3

Twin-Seater

- Size - 60" long x 25" deep x 35" tall
- Classic outdoor design
- Convenient table incorporated into this unique design
- Complete list of materials
- Step-by-step instructions

Plan #DM2-002D-0005

Price Code P3

Picnic Bench and Table

- Table size - 6'-0" x 5'-2"
- Bench size - 6'-0" x 2'-7"
- Converts from table to bench
- Wood cutting diagrams to help you cut cost
- Sturdy construction
- Complete list of materials
- Step-by-step instructions

Plan #DM2-002D-0007

Price Code P3

Fences and Gates - 9 Designs

- Nine popular designs to select from
- Ideas for security, privacy and beauty
- From wood framing to chain link fencing
- Guides to help you estimate, buy and build
- Complete list of materials
- Step-by-step instructions

Plan #DM2-066D-0008

Price Code P3

Folding Adirondack Chair

- Size - 24" x 39" x 37" high
- Good looking and comfortable
- Folds up in one motion
- Full-size traceable patterns
- Complete list of materials
- Step-by-step instructions

To order online visit www.projecplans.com

Plan #DM2-002D-0003

Price Code P3

Picnic Tables

- Two popular styles -
    Rectangle - 72" x 60" x 30" high
    Octagon - 56" x 56" x 30" high
- Ideal for outdoor entertaining and backyard barbecues
- Complete list of materials
- Step-by-step instructions

Plan #DM2-002D-0004

Price Code P3

Adirondack Chair

- Size - 66" x 27" x 40" high
- A project that's very practical and unique
- Two piece set
- Sturdy construction
- Complete list of materials
- Step-by-step instructions

Plan #DM2-002D-0006

Price Code P3

Patio Furniture - 3 Piece Set

- Lounge seat - 63" x 32" x 31" high
- Ideal for patio or deck
- Convenient for outdoor entertaining
- Complete list of materials
- Step-by-step instructions

Plan #DM2-002D-0014

Price Code P3

All-Purpose Bench

- Size - 72" x 20" x 36" high
- Enhance your garden, patio or deck
- Complements any setting
- Complete list of materials
- Step-by-step instructions

Plan #DM2-002D-0015

Price Code P3

Porch Swing

- Size - 72" x 24" x 26" high
- Ideal for attaching to porch or any outdoor structure
- Attractive and sturdy design
- Complete list of materials
- Step-by-step instructions

Plan #DM2-066D-0001

Price Code P3

Tree Seat

- Easily adjusts to fit most trees
- Full-size traceable patterns
- Complete list of materials
- Step-by-step instructions

To order online visit www.projectplans.com

Construction Blueprints...

FULLY DETAILED BLUEPRINTS AVAILABLE
for all projects featured in this book.

Blueprint Plans include the following:

- A complete list of materials
- Fully dimensioned details

- Framing plans
- Framing elevations

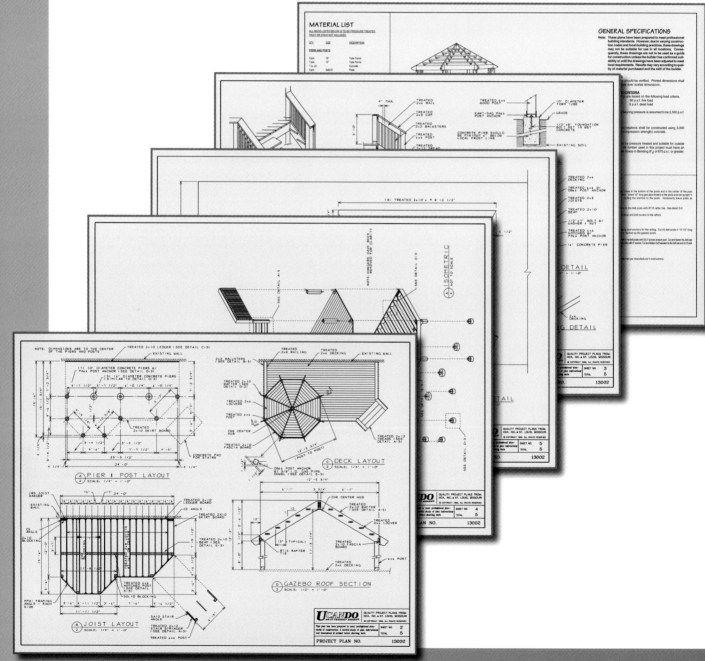

Project Plan Index

Design No.	Price Code	Page	Reproducibles Available	Design No.	Price Code	Page	Reproducibles Available
DM2-002D-0003	P3	76	X	DM2-002D-3024	P4	69	X
DM2-002D-0004	P3	76	X	DM2-002D-3025	P5	66	X
DM2-002D-0005	P3	75	X	DM2-002D-3026	P5	61	X
DM2-002D-0006	P3	76	X	DM2-002D-3027	P4	49	X
DM2-002D-0007	P3	75	X	DM2-002D-3028	P3	70	X
DM2-002D-0012	P3	74	X	DM2-002D-3029	P6	60	X
DM2-002D-0013	P3	72	X	DM2-063D-3000	P6	63	
DM2-002D-0014	P3	77	X	DM2-063D-3001	P4	64	
DM2-002D-0015	P3	77	X	DM2-063D-3002	P6	61	
DM2-002D-3000	P6	64	X	DM2-063D-3003	P6	63	
DM2-002D-3001	P6	60	X	DM2-063D-3004	P6	62	
DM2-002D-3002	P4	51	X	DM2-064D-3000	P6	65	X
DM2-002D-3003	P5	70	X	DM2-064D-3001	P6	65	X
DM2-002D-3004	P3	50	X	DM2-064D-3002	P5	56	X
DM2-002D-3005	P4	52	X	DM2-064D-3003	P5	56	X
DM2-002D-3006	P4	55	X	DM2-064D-3004	P3	57	X
DM2-002D-3007	P5	54	X	DM2-064D-3005	P4	57	X
DM2-002D-3008	P5	67	X	DM2-064D-3006	P4	58	X
DM2-002D-3009	P4	55	X	DM2-064D-3007	P4	58	X
DM2-002D-3010	P5	54	X	DM2-064D-3008	P6	59	X
DM2-002D-3011	P3	52	X	DM2-064D-3009	P6	59	X
DM2-002D-3012	P3	69	X	DM2-066D-0001	P3	77	X
DM2-002D-3013	P4	71	X	DM2-066D-0006	P3	73	X
DM2-002D-3014	P4	66	X	DM2-066D-0008	P3	75	X
DM2-002D-3015	P4	68	X	DM2-066D-0018	P3	74	X
DM2-002D-3016	P5	53	X	DM2-066D-0019	P3	72	X
DM2-002D-3017	P5	68	X	DM2-066D-0020	P3	73	X
DM2-002D-3018	P5	62	X	DM2-066D-0021	P3	72	X
DM2-002D-3019	P5	53	X	DM2-066D-0022	P3	74	X
DM2-002D-3020	P5	48	X	DM2-066D-0023	P3	73	X
DM2-002D-3021	P4	51	X	DM2-102D-3000	P6	67	X
DM2-002D-3022	P3	71	X	DM2-107D-3001	P5	48	X
DM2-002D-3023	P5	49	X	DM2-107D-3002	P4	50	X

How To Order

**For fastest service, Call Toll-Free
1-800-DREAM HOME
(1-800-373-2646) day or night**

FOUR Easy Ways To Order

1. CALL toll-free 1-800-373-2646 for credit card orders. MasterCard, Visa, Discover and American Express are accepted.

2. FAX your order to 1-314-770-2226.

3. MAIL the Order Form to:

   **HDA, Inc.
   944 Anglum Road
   St. Louis, MO 63042
   Attn: Customer Service Dept.**

4. ONLINE visit www.projectplans.com

QUESTIONS?
**Call Our Customer Service Number
314-770-2228**

Order Form

Please send me -

PLAN NUMBER DM2- _____

PRICE CODE _____ (see Plan Page)

Reproducible Masters (see index for availability) $ _____
One-Set of Plans $ _____
Additional Plan Sets (see chart at right)
_____ (Qty) at $10 each $ _____

                             SUBTOTAL $ _____
SALES TAX (MO residents add 6%) $ _____
☐ Shipping / Handling (see chart at right) $ _____
   (each additional set add $2.00 to shipping charges)

TOTAL ENCLOSED (US funds only) $ _____

☐ Enclosed is my check or money order payable to HDA, Inc. (Sorry, no COD's)

I hereby authorize HDA, Inc. to charge this purchase to my credit card account (check one):

☐ MasterCard ☐ VISA ☐ DISCOVER ☐ AMERICAN EXPRESS Cards

Credit Card number_____

Expiration date_____

Signature _____

Name_____
          (Please print or type)

Street Address_____
          *(Please **do not** use PO Box)*

City _____

State _____   Zip _____

Daytime phone number (_____) - _____

E-mail _____

Important Information to Know Before You Order

♦ **Exchange Policies -** Since blueprints are printed in response to your order, we cannot honor requests for refunds. However, if for some reason you find that the plan you have purchased does not meet your requirements, you may exchange that plan for another plan in our collection within 90 days of purchase. At the time of the exchange, you will be charged a processing fee of 25% of your original plan package price, plus the difference in price between the plan packages (if applicable) and the cost to ship the new plans to you.

Please note: *Reproducible drawings can only be exchanged if the package is unopened.*

♦ **Building Codes & Requirements -** At the time the construction drawings were prepared, every effort was made to ensure that these plans and specifications meet nationally recognized codes. Our plans conform to most national building codes. Because building codes vary from area to area, some drawing modifications and/or the assistance of a professional designer or architect may be necessary to comply with your local codes or to accommodate specific building site conditions. We advise you to consult with your local building official for information regarding codes governing your area.

Blueprint Price Schedule

Price Code	1-Set	Additional Sets	Reproducible Masters
P3	$15.00	$10.00	$65.00
P4	$20.00	$10.00	$70.00
P5	$25.00	$10.00	$75.00
P6	$30.00	$10.00	$80.00

**Plan prices subject to change without notice.
Please note that plans are not refundable.**

Shipping & Handling Charges
EACH ADDITIONAL SET ADD $2.00 TO SHIPPING CHARGES

U.S. SHIPPING - (AK and HI express only)

Regular *(allow 7-10 business days)* $5.95
Priority *(allow 3-5 business days)* $15.00
Express* *(allow 1-2 business days)* $25.00

CANADA SHIPPING**

Standard *(allow 8-12 business days)* $15.00
Express* *(allow 3-5 business days)* $40.00

OVERSEAS SHIPPING/INTERNATIONAL
Call, fax, or e-mail (plans@hdainc.com) for shipping costs.

* For express delivery please call us by 11:00 a.m. Monday-Friday CST

** Orders may be subject to custom's fees and or duties/taxes.